THE WELL

Parables for Living and Dying

This book is due for return on or before the last date indicated on label. Renewals may be obtained on application.

242

First published in 1996 by
Darton, Longman and Todd Ltd
1 Spencer Court
140–142 Wandsworth High Street
London SW18 4JJ

ISBN 0–232–52172–7

A catalogue record for this book is available
from the British Library

Phototypeset in 10½/12½ Baskerville by Intype London Limited
Printed and bound in Great Britain by
Redwood Books Ltd, Trowbridge, Wiltshire

Contents

Dedicated with the greatest affection and gratitude to the people of Dinnington – to friends and family, carers and congregation, and to the wider parish – for support and solidarity that enables me to go on 'living in the face of dying'.

So by this infirmity may I be protected, by this completed. So in this darkness may I be clothed in light.

JOHN MILTON

Part I

AN INTRODUCTORY REFLECTION

LIVING IN THE FACE OF DYING

IT WAS Remembrance Day – I certainly remember it, 11 November 1985. I had been on retreat in Durham and returned home. I never unpack my bags before I've looked through the post and so, sitting among the luggage, I found a letter from the hospital. I had been undergoing tests to discover why my blood took so long to clot. The letter simply said I needed to contact the hospital urgently. It was as vague as that but I knew. I hadn't really thought about it seriously until then but somehow I knew. The dread – even then in 1985 – of every gay man. HTLV III, as they called it then, the HIV virus that leads to AIDS. I knew very little about it, neither really did anybody else, but it hovered already, rightly or wrongly, as the great fear of the gay community. And now they were going to tell me it was there in my blood.

My journal says:

> And after that to return home to the sudden possi-
> bility – I don't think I'm being melodramatic – of
> death . . . I'm terribly self-conscious, self-aware,
> febrile, shaking. . . .

And then it goes on:

> And the lust to live is incredibly strong – an angry
> strength: I have just too much, too many people, to
> live for. . . .

I danced. On my own, in amongst the luggage and the

other unopened mail, I put on a favourite record and danced:

'I keep dancing', says the journal, 'a kind of frenzy, the liveliest thing I can do. . . .'

The diagnosis was confirmed a week later at the hospital and I, fit and healthy and well, found myself from then on living in the face of dying.

We are of course, all of us 'living in the face of dying', there is no surer fact, but none of us is very good at it. And to know you are carrying with you a deadly virus doesn't mean you know what to do with it. For me, knowing about this deadly thing inside me but continuing to be fit and well for many years after the diagnosis only made things more difficult. I had no idea what to do with this 'information' about myself. I would look at it, hold it up, walk round it – 'you might soon be dead' – but somehow it didn't sink in. At other times I could even forget about it completely. There were the times too, of course, when suddenly it would overwhelm me.

'I do things', says the journal, 'and suddenly something sinks away – the possibility, it yawns and gapes, an abyss.'

I felt of course, as someone who tries to pray, that I ought to be able to face this. At least to begin, to try, but the constant image from those first years living with the virus is of a brick wall, an impenetrable wilderness. I might frequently return to face the question but for so long it was simply facing a wall, staring into nothing at all.

To begin with I hoped – almost assumed – I was one of those who, they were saying then, would not progress to AIDS. The sinking feeling returned more strongly and more forcefully as, after about seven years, my immune system began to show the clearer signs of deterioration.

Then I began to lose weight, to have to live with diarrhoea, to find eating difficult. I had not escaped.

As I became more visibly ill it became necessary to talk to others – so far I had kept it almost completely secret. It became even more necessary to talk to myself, to step out into the wilderness. One of the ways I found to do that – talking to myself and to others – was to tell 'stories'. And that is what this book in the end is about. It was not a conscious 'scheme' and developed only slowly but three things seem to have moved forward together and I have come to feel they are intimately linked. The three twined things are the progress of the illness, my readiness to begin to find ways of talking with others about my 'affliction', and the telling of 'stories'.

Mohammed is said to have told those who were rebuking a man for groaning in agony: 'Let him groan, for groaning also is one of the names of God.'[1]

I realise now that in many ways my 'brick wall' was partly to do with refusing to accept affliction, denying it and being afraid. The fear has not gone entirely but I have moved somehow forward into the wilderness and am able, sometimes at least, to 'groan honestly' before God. I begin to be able to 'live with' the illness rather than denying it and begin to face some of the questions it brings. Affliction, pain especially, (though I fortunately have had little pain so far) can be obliterating. It can take away the desire, the sheer ability, to do anything but suffer. At other times though it powerfully peels away pretence and shallow evasion and confronts us with the sharp and deep questions. Affliction pushes the fundamental questions of spirituality:

1. The Koran.

Who are you really?
What do you really want?
Where really are you going?
What really are you afraid of?

There is at last a desire to be as openly and simply honest as possible – with oneself, with the world – no more pretence, no more secrets, deceptions and self-deceptions. What would be the point? In the face of dying life itself comes vividly alive, loses its accretions and superficialities and becomes a sharp and fiercely clear reality. Thin ambitions, wasted time and energy, shallowness, fall away and you are left with this lovely, essential beautiful thing – life, so precious, so fragile.

I realise, of course, that this is not true for everyone. Confronting a life-threatening illness for some people leads simply to an enduring panic, a permanent sense of disaster, a conviction that life is even more horrible and unfair than ever you thought before. There seems to be little rhyme or reason as to why some react one way and others so differently. Religious faith does not necessarily make a difference – that despairing reaction can afflict anyone but it has not, so far, afflicted me. For me it is more as if the clutter and the unnecessary accretions have been removed and I am left for now with a clearer sense of the rich beauty of life. It is accompanied by a powerful sense of grace – of the sheer 'givenness', 'giftedness' of it all, undeserved, unsought, something beautiful and good. Of course in a sense this now becomes so fragile, so delicate to hold, so likely to be lost but as a foundation, a bottom of the well, it certainly for now constitutes a strong place from which to attempt to be honest, a security in which to face those 'basic questions' we all should face.

6

Illness, especially terminal illness, provides a kind of enforced space in which to face those questions but the desire to be honest in prayer about ourselves and before God should perhaps lead us to choose a space from time to time in which to ask the questions. And it will be more than once because this kind of searching honesty is a process, not a single event. In a sense the questions have no single answers but they probe the basic facets of ourselves, facets which change and develop and grow. For me in this context, the keeping of a journal has been of increasing importance. It has not involved daily entries necessarily, but frequently records my attempts to face these questions – and records too the evasions and self-deceptions. Somehow the act of writing down my reactions obliges a greater honesty and reviewing the journals reveals the developments, however slow, as well, sometimes, as the continuing deceptions. The human being is very skilled in self-deception and all of us tend to let our honest responses be smothered over, masked and concealed. Inevitably then we need to turn regularly to this invitation to be honest. In a rather different way that act of writing which leads to honesty is a motivation in creating the stories of this book, presenting answers to the questions for which there seem otherwise to be no suitable words.

The questions again:

> Who really am I?
> What do I really want?
> Where am I really going?
> What really am I afraid of?

This is not, of course, an invitation to the frantic self-examination of the merely self-accusing kind, guilt-ridden and self-absorbed as that inevitably will be. Rather it should be a contemplative kind of gazing inwards which begins or extends the journey of spirit, which is an opening up and a blossoming not only towards greater inner integration but also, and inevitably linked to that, greater integration with others in personal relationships and in wider sympathies. The questions press a finger against the nature of my identity, then the nature of my deepest desires, then the nature of my sense of destiny, then the nature of my dignity . . . together they invite me to see a whole person, blossoming in integrity, appropriately self-assured but also aware of the worlds of other people, open to them and ready, brave enough to keep growing whatever the future holds.

Identity. Desire. Destiny. Dignity:

I am a person in my own right, not merely dependent on others. I can stand up straight and be myself with others without self-centredness or arrogance but in quiet assurance and integrity. From such a stance I can begin to love unselfishly and without possessiveness.

My hopes and longings for myself and for those around me, for my world, have integrity and deserve recognition. I can work to penetrate the more shallow desires that are merely superficial and reach that place of deeper longing and broader hope where what I desire begins to be integrated with the wider human world and the deepest of shared longings.

I can begin to discern a pattern and a shape to my life which has greater purpose and meaning. It does involve my choices and decisions, made with clear thought and with respect for others but it also acknowledges a sense of 'calling' that is specific to me and to which I must be honest and loyal. There will be mistakes too, wrong turnings taken and even sometimes a willing blindness but I can turn and begin again.

8

There is nothing I need to fear – in myself or from the world. I can live in dignity with courage and face whatever seems to threaten. I am not in isolation from the world, alone and fearful, but can share love with others and discover the love that streams in the universe. If I acknowledge the profound dignity of every human being, however sometimes distorted, then I affirm my own dignity too and enter a world without fear or loneliness.

Inevitably the process of gazing inwards like this will expose all the things that get in the way and they may not all be movable at once. It is a journey and a process. W. H. Auden said: 'The desires of the heart are as crooked as corkscrews' and responding to the questions may mean following all down those twists and turns until something straighter can be uncovered. We pose and we wear masks as much to hide from ourselves as from others. All kinds of fears get in the way, so often quite unrecognised as fears. By choosing to seek this kind of honesty, all these things are steadily penetrated and slowly begin to move away. The journey doesn't end but once begun it becomes a kind of hunger, a longing that is hard to suppress, so that it feels like standing up straight in sunlight after being crouched, cramped in a low dark tunnel. . . .

It feels like a journey towards a place in the universe, achieving a sense of balance about myself and my place in the world, a sense of proportion and equilibrium. It is about how much I, and my attempts to be honest, matter to God on the one hand and on the other, how tiny and insignificant I am on the cosmic scale. Equally it is about recognising too the tininess of the earth and of the 'human adventure' in that same scale and yet, again, how that matters to God. So my integrity includes my integration into the flow and flux of this vast universe, its ageless, seemingly undifferentiated continuity and the fleck there of my contribution, as honest and true as I can make it. A 'fleck' and yet it seems somehow precious and delightful in its very tininess in a universe which is a mutual interdependence of tininesses.

The best word, in many ways, for this desired sense of balance and equilibrium is 'disinterest' though sadly its meaning is becoming lost and corrupted. It somehow has a cold and distant air to it but it should be heard to mean a proper sense of detachment, without clinging and grasping. It is about a non-possessiveness with regard both to material things but also to the affections and commitments of other people. Clinging need becomes instead disinterested love. It is also a non-possessiveness about my own destiny too – the end of a sense of desperation about 'where I shall be' or 'what will happen next?' It does not mean a lack of commitment in relationships or a loss of interest in life itself, rather, with the rubble and debris cleared away, there is the possibility of a steady clarity of disinterested commitment, even perhaps a kind of 'passionate disinterest'. This seems to me to be precisely the kind of attitude Jesus had reached – through the Last Supper, through Gethsemane – by the time he reached his trial. His silence was not a loss of interest, not fear or panic or mere resignation, but the courageous integrity of disinterested love, passionately disinterested love.

For me, the pattern so clear in Jesus is also the shape of the universe, that 'disinterested love' lies behind the 'mutual interdependence of tininesses'. Donald Nicholl, writing in *The Tablet* some years ago, quoted a beautiful picture of this connectedness and mutuality:

> Consider Indira's net – the vivid symbol which is used as an aid to meditation in Kegon Buddhism. This great imaginary net is to be visualised as stretch-

ing throughout the entire universe, its vertical extension representing time and its horizontal extension
representing space. At every point where the net's
threads interconnect one is asked to imagine a crystal
bead symbolising an individual existence. Each one
of these innumerable crystals reflects on its own surface not only every other bead in the net but every
reflection of every other bead, thus creating number-
less, endless reflections of each other while forming
the complete and total whole.

So for me, responding to the questions leads to this vision
of a universe of integrity into which I fit, with or without
affliction. I discover the goodness and beauty of the universe and it seems to me essentially ready to affirm my
attempt, all our attempts, to be honest. At its very bottom,
endless though it is, it is positive and creative, living and
growing healthily, somehow able to soak up and transform
affliction, pain and evil.

But the question presses itself again. Is this a merely
arbitrary choice of belief? Why believe all this rather than
that the universe is cold, meaningless, faceless and ulti-
mately chaotic?

There is inevitably something arbitrary in the choice of
belief and yet the choice is made in the context of my
experience. For me there is something not-to-be-contra-
dicted about the facts of beauty and goodness in the world
– beauty in the stuff of the universe itself, in the earth and
in humanity itself too. There is something inescapable
too in our ability to create beauty and goodness so I find myself effectively 'trapped' by its irrefutable reality: I couldn't
deny it even if I wanted to. Over against the coldest,
pseudo-scientific mechanistic analyses of the universe I
see the reality of beauty and goodness and I cannot escape.

This 'Beauty and Goodness' streams for me in everything, and includes me in my tiny place, it is sometimes concealed, not least by evil and affliction, but it is so often breathtakingly visible and yet still ignored, and sometimes it is quite unignorable – to it I give the name of 'God'. I find the sightline of vision towards this God is cleansed and cleared by responding to the questions explored earlier but many who experience affliction of different kinds find in quite other ways, and by their own routes, that this beauty and goodness becomes ever more unignorable.

There is for many then, who live with the prospect of dying this powerful attractiveness about the life they are now at risk of losing. Over against the affliction and the fear (but maybe somehow through them too) I have experienced an intense beauty, stronger than ever I knew before. I had always felt, with Dostoevsky, that 'beauty will save the world'. Now I seem to know that in the most intense way. The beauty of the world itself is overwhelming – of water, rain, waterfalls and the sea, of trees and islands and mountains. Simple colours have taken on a vivid intensity, in flowers, in paintings, yellow, saffron, cobalt blue. And human beauty too, created beauty in poetry and painting and music – Bach's cello suites, Mozart's *Magic Flute* but also vibrant dance music like that first urgent celebration of life after the fateful letter, though now sadly I no longer have the energy actually to dance. There is a sharp reality to it all, beautiful and vivid like Thomas Traherne's *Centuries*:

> The green trees when I saw them first through one of the gates transported and ravished me; their sweetness and unusual beauty made my heart to leap, and

almost mad with ecstasy, they were such strange
and wonderful things.[2]

This human beauty of created things embraces the makers
too. Traherne continues:

> The men! O what venerable and reverend creatures
> did the aged seem! Immortal cherubims! And young
> men glittering and sparkling angels, and maids
> strange seraphic pieces of life and beauty! Boys and
> girls tumbling in the street and playing were moving
> jewels.

And for me too there is a new beauty in people – my
mother, my sisters and brother, my friends, people who
have shown their care for me in affliction, parishioners,
those who faithfully take it in turns to stay with me night
by night during my intravenous treatment, people who
have contacted me since my story was televised by the
BBC.[3] Relationships remind me more than anything else
that there is no time to waste, life is precious, beautiful, to
be celebrated, lived intensely with honesty and integrity.

This 'human beauty' includes my own body too. That
may seem odd since my body was becoming thinner, less
agile, my face more gaunt. But the journal records: 'This
is my body – I love it, I want it; I'm not proud of it but
I'm not ashamed of it either: I want to cherish it, to hold
it, hold on to it. I feel sad for it with this "presence"
inside of it – it's mine, it's me, I love it. . . .'

Wounded and afflicted it might be but to love its unique
beauty was to find a kind of healing. I am frequently
reminded of some words of Nikos Kazantzakis, quoted
amongst the Cairns for the Journey in Jim Cotter's *Prayer*

2. Thomas Traherne, *Selected Writing* (Carcanet Press, 1980).
3. 'Simon's Cross', BBC *Everyman* series, 15 January 1995.

at Night:[4] 'Deep down in the bowels of everyone there lives a horrible unclean larva. Lean over and say to this larva, I love you, and it will sprout wings and become a butterfly'.

In a very specific sense for me the 'larva' is the virus. I find it impossibly hard to love this particular enemy. Writers have spoken of 'befriending' cancers and deadly diseases. My own spiritual director talked with me about living with the virus rather than against it and always consciously taking it, and all whom it affects, with me to the altar at the eucharist, a strange kind of offering. If I can somehow 'live alongside' this thing inside me then somehow my body can have a certain kind of beauty in acceptance, whatever it looks like to the world. This would be 'living in the face of dying'.

There is, however, nothing frantic about all this, no sense of desperation: it does not seem to be based on a desire to cling possessively to what I can, while I can, a fear of loss. I seem to live with very little fear of that kind. The journal early on quotes G. K. Chesterton: 'One should leave nothing in the world of which one is afraid.' And steadily now I seem to have got nearer to that.

It is in this sense of a beauty in life and in the middle of a steadily developing illness that the 'stories' begin to appear, tentative expressions of the affliction and the beauty.

The mind has many levels. A human being operates in many different ways. A Russian *staretz* said: 'Prayer is to stand before God with the mind in the heart.'

Instead of the brick wall I seemed now at last to begin to descend with my mind into my heart and to begin to be able to touch and handle my experience, to explore

4. Jim Cotter, *Prayer at Night* (Cairns Publications, 1983).

it, to speak of it: to myself, to others, even to God. A beginning anyway.

Another word for 'the mind in the heart' might be 'imagination' – in any case these tentative explorations formed as images, as metaphors, as 'stories'. The journal in 1992 says this: 'I begin to "metaphor-ise" everything but that seems to me like perceiving the numinous, opening the doors of perception . . . even "God" is a metaphor, after all.'

The first 'story' to be written was about the wilderness (p. 40), about finally stepping into its deserted emptiness. I wrote it for myself but I wrote it also to use in a worship group – a way of speaking from my mind in my heart, a way of praying. This is a world below the reasoning head. That part of me is so culture-bound, so logical, so memory-conditioned, so ready with answers, but I needed a way of speaking from below that, to myself and to others.

I had felt for some time a need to descend to this level: it pictured itself in me as a well with a great stone lid almost completely covering the rim of the well. A tiny gap remained which told me there really was fresh deep clear water way down below in me. A water of 'images', a well of 'stories'. I felt I could, I needed to, push that lid off the well and reach down for the water. This was a way then of facing the questions I could not find any other way of facing. It was one response, at least, to the brick wall. I could push the lid off the well.

Metaphors seem to be given, they write themselves. They write themselves into, up against and out of those fundamental questions of spirituality: Who are you? Where are you going?. . . A woman in the West of Ireland has written to me ever since the television programme and become a friend. For my fortieth birthday she told me she had planted a tree for me in a Galway forest.

Immediately the echoes began, the tree resonated as a metaphor, a picture for me of life and growth, renewal, absorption in the forest: the image was given, the 'story' grew. This for me is George Herbert's 'Christian plummet sounding heav'n and earth' – touching the bottom of the well, interpreting the depths.

My wilderness became more specifically 'Australia'. I had not consciously been reading books about that continent but again the metaphor was 'given' when I read a book about the aborigine 'dream time', *Creation Spirituality and the Dreamtime,* edited by Catherine Hammond.[5] It touched off a connecting-up of other books – the novels of Patrick White, Bruce Chatwin's *Songlines*[6] and more recently *Remembering Babylon* by David Malouf.[7] From there emerged this powerful sense of a vast empty unexplored interior – a wilderness – with 'civilised' living clinging to its fringes, its edges, and yet with a dream time too and, waiting to be discovered, those songlines that lead the way through the desert. I was facing the 'outback', the interior of my Australia and the inviting songlines were the 'stories'.

I keep putting inverted commas around the term 'stories' because it is not the right word for what I have constructed. I cannot however find another one. 'Fables' will not quite do because it has too much of a moral overtone, 'myth' is a bit too grand but these stories are perhaps

5. Catherine Hammond (ed.), *Creation Spirituality and the Dreamtime* (Millennium Books, 1991).
6. Bruce Chatwin, *The Songlines* (Jonathan Cape, 1987).
7. David Malouf, *Remembering Babylon* (Chatto & Windus, 1993).

part of the same world. 'Parables' is problematic too. What I have written are extended images of our explorations, developed metaphors for inner experience. The great myths of ancient cultures like Greece or India are mirrors for the interior life of humanity; as psychology has shown they are archetypes. Often the stories have a dream-like quality and, in fact, for me some of them are directly derived from dreams. My dreams have changed. My family – my mother, three sisters and brother – appear frequently in ways they never used to do. School and college and friends from those days – some of them long-forgotten – appear, there is some kind of return, of life completing a circle. There is surging water and winding paths and most numinous of all a small child, fair, often silent – I know him but can't quite remember his name . . .

Among the world's stories most powerful for me personally are the myths of our own islands – of King Arthur and of the Celts. As a child it was King Arthur I loved but any stories would do, including those we told each other as children especially when we were all put together in one warm bedroom because we all had mumps or some other ailment – I think we even had a literal 'magic carpet' to sit on in front of the fire! Growing up did not mean leaving stories behind but developed into a love of novels, old and new, including the study of them at university. All those stories, childish; modern novels; ancient tales, demonstrate a widely recognised desire in us to find images for our experience, and not just pictures but narratives, whole stories to shape our perception of the world. Different cultures produce different expressions and they grow and die away within cultures too. As I contemplated 'telling stories', part of the consideration was to explore the images which resonated for me specifically, and for my world. Simply re-telling old folk tales was

17

not enough, powerful as they can be. The images needed to arise from within – in me and where I am. So they needed to be shared images too with which others would immediately resonate also. The journey, the path, the way, the light and the dark, deserts, seeds and growth, the house, the well, the river, the sea, the mountain – all these might stir echoes.

Another of the spurs to pursue this idea was the remark by a member of our congregation who said, 'We need new parables'. Stories in a Christian milieu are inevitably coloured by the rich and vivid pattern of the parables of Jesus. He knew the power of the image, the depths which a metaphor might touch, the echoes he could stir in people with his searching stories: treasure in a field, a rising loaf of bread, a huge catch of fish, a seed scattered abroad, a determined woman before a lazy judge, a lost son and a running father. . . . It surprises me that the history of Christianity isn't full of more and more parables, emulating Jesus. Perhaps we have been too awed by his extraordinary example, unable to compete – or perhaps the history of Western arts is just such a variation on his theme. . . . Whatever may be the case his exuberant fountain of metaphors cannot have been intended as a completed canon. (How deadening that sounds!) He invites us to go on making comparisons, finding images, exploring new pictures, making our own parables: 'God is like this . . . like that . . . God's new world is like this . . .'

It is instructive to look more closely at how parables work and the 'technique' Jesus, in particular, used in telling them. The heart of the parable is an image derived from shared experience. Most obviously the source was the contemporary social world and its established structures that Jesus could take for granted with his hearers – masters and servants, kings and courts, judges

18

and suppliants. It might be more domestic – fathers and sons, a wedding, sowing seed or tending sheep. It might relate to even more basic feelings and attitudes – hunger, greed, indebtedness, desire. It might have a sharper edge – Pharisees and a publican, thieves, foreigners – or make a religious connection in a more subtle way like the parable of the Vineyard, echoing a familiar story and yet subtly and devastatingly different. The image is planted in the minds of the hearers, in their imagination, and then, one way or another, the link is made with God.

The point of the parable is in that link to God and for those first hearers the association must often have come as a shock, a puzzle – what connection could there be between God and this image? How could God be thought of in this way? The reaction is not necessarily a violent one though sometimes it must have been: for Jesus to affirm the publican at his prayers rather than the so-religious Pharisee must have been a real shock. But at other times the reaction is a kind of awakening. The image opens something up – the treasure buried in the field, the pearl of great price – so that is what it's like. . . . There is a 'cleansing of the doors of perception', an exposure to a whole new world of ideas and imagination. This is surely at the heart of the *metanoia*, the repentance, that Jesus announced as crucial for this new world, an opening up, a turning round, a turning inside out and upside down. It would begin to work away like yeast in a loaf of bread.

It also, however, might *not* begin to work like that . . . there do seem to be those who do not 'have ears to hear', those who cannot make the connection of the images. Where does the faculty for perceiving metaphor come from? Is it innate in everyone, waiting to be uncovered, or will some never make the connection? It clearly *can*

be deeply buried but would in some senses seem to be
something 'given' to us in the nature of being human. It
can be something very difficult to teach and to that extent,
and in many other ways, it is close to the nature of language itself. Words themselves, after all, are metaphors or
symbols representing objects and experiences. At college
I helped for a while in a local primary school in a class
of small children just beginning to learn to read. I worked
for some weeks on my regular day there with a little boy
having particular difficulty getting started. We looked at
a picture of a swan underneath which was written the
word 'swan' and he would recognise the picture, 'a swan'.
When I asked him 'what "swan" began with', 'what was
the first letter', he had no idea what I meant. He had no
concept of 'swan' as a word only as a bird in a picture we
were looking at. The moment of connection had not yet
arrived – I was not there when it did but he must soon
have come to link those squiggly lines under the picture
with the bird and seen that the one represented the other,
just as the sound he made with his mouth in recognising
the picture was also a 'metaphor' for the swan. It would
have dawned on him, as in a similar way, the world of
parables and stories, metaphors and images may only
slowly 'dawn on' us as central to the life of spirit. This
world of the imagination lies behind all symbols and sacra-
ments and images, behind ritual and ceremonial too, and
so is essential to religion and spirituality. To cultivate it –
in ourselves as in others – is vital, even if sometimes it
means letting the yeast work slowly, even for years, until
the 'ears can hear'.

It is not necessarily meant to be an easier way into the
world of spirit, though it may be a way to go deeper. In
fact some of the stories of Jesus seem to be deliberately
difficult. (That may of course only be the form in which

we've received them.) It is as if we are intended to take the story away and savour it, chew and puzzle over it, work to make its connections. Sometimes, surely, we take the stories too seriously and fail to catch what must have been the amused, ironic tone in Jesus's voice, his tongue in his cheek. Giving scorpions to our children, nagging widows, thieves in the night, dramatically harsh kings. . . . The solemn intonation of some of these parables read as the Gospel in church contrasts sharply and amusingly with how they must have been told originally. The riot of images and the abundance of stories tumbling from the lips of Jesus must often have been more like the joke-telling of *Godspell*: 'I say, I say, I say . . .'; 'Have you heard the one about. . . ?'

The whole technique itself was an innovation. This religious teacher doing so much of his work by telling unexplained stories must have been a shock and a disturbance, if not actually threatening, to his contemporaries. Stories could be so accessible to everyone. Moreover, left uninterpreted, they invited people to respond personally and to think for themselves whilst at the same time all entering into the common world of the story's images. On the other hand there was also a clear tradition of prophetic storytelling and a kind of propensity for it in the Jewish character. It simply blossomed here into a rich flowering. It connected too with one of the most widespread means of the human communication of meaning, information, purpose, pleasure and longing. Jesus used this means supremely to say all that for which he otherwise had no words, his parable-telling coming to its devastating climax in the acted-out parable of the cross.

His stories were about God. They begin in the Gospel records with the euphemistic phrases 'the kingdom of heaven is like . . .' or 'the kingdom of God is like . . .', but this new world he speaks of is the world of the God whose character and purposes in their fullness and richness he is struggling to convey to his hearers. So the themes of his stories are constantly about this God who urgently seeks us out when we are lost, who gives himself to us in unequalled and extravagant generosity. The stories invite us always to be ready and alert for God giving himself to us at any moment, to be awake and aware. They are about the sheer preciousness of the human being, 'great' or 'humble', and the constant divine reversal of our assumptions here. And the stories are full too of a sense of the divine purposes carefully working themselves out, despite all appearances, towards the great and final arrival of this new world full of love and justice and hope. By implication, and sometimes explicitly, the new world of these stories is set over against the rule-regulated, stale and institutionalised world of conventional religion. That world need not be impervious to the new world as Nicodemus, for instance, demonstrates. Coming as a representative of the 'old world' to Jesus he finds himself invited, by the mysterious 'story' of being born again, to enter that new world and he makes his choice. With that picture, as in every parable, Jesus opens up the possibility of life that nothing can defeat. He celebrates the gift in overflowing full measure of this earth-shattering new world, the overwhelming presence there – here – of goodness, beauty, life. Like a priceless jewel, like the treasure for which you would give everything you have.

For me this deep-seated inclination in Jesus continually to search for pictures and stories to try to embody what he wants to say comes to its climax at the Last Supper where, in contemplating this last meal with his friends, he makes for them the deepest connection of all between himself and their life together 'pictorially' shared in the meal. As he breaks the bread for them and offers them the cup of wine he unerringly ensures that always there they will re-member ('put together again', as it were) his life, his love, 'My Body', 'My Blood'. In those single words the whole action is transformed into a story, into something far deeper than a parable, into a celebration of the life of the new world opened up for everyone.

I faced the interior of 'Australia' with none of this thought through in any systematic way but the brick wall, the wilderness, had become a place to enter – a wasteland of affliction still but with the chance of Songlines.

Songlines are said to be the trails across the waste interior of Australia which enable the aborigines to find their way for thousands of miles. They are known by song, melodies that resonate for the native and lead the way. I like the idea that in the history of language for the human race music and song and poetry came first. First the singing sounds of the voice and then the development of meaning, grammar and detail – but all of it communication. Someone said:

> 'Poetry is the mother tongue of the human race as the garden is older than the field, painting than writing, singing than declaiming, parables than inferences, bartering than commerce . . .'

Finding stories to tell is a writing that tries to return to that primitive, deep and original communication. It can be like poetry, like songs, like Songlines. (An editor at DLT in writing to me about this book inadvertently referred to the 'poems' rather than the 'stories'.)

Still though a sharper question remains. The 'stories'

may be trying to approach 'deep and original communication' but can they really face death? Can the imagination deal with this brick wall? Is there a 'story of death'? I have felt it like a void and written that story, I have felt something of its sheer emptiness, the 'nothing' that is there. It is surely what Jesus faced, abandoned and alone, as he was dying on the cross. I have come to feel that the reality of that must be fully faced, however hard and numbing, if life itself is to be free to have its fullest meaning. But it is so elusive, so difficult to articulate. The ego ends – but that is not the end of 'life'. Somehow it's the beginning. Stumbling in search of what this means I wrote in my journal:

> This is not specific to AIDS but maybe you can in fact 'live with', live into, dying itself. Any terminal illness asks you to face death but maybe those of us in such situations – if we can – have a chance, maybe even a vocation, a special privilege – to say that you can live with dying too. It's not the ultimate horror, the great devil, the fear can be transfigured if you dare to live honestly alongside it.

And the phrase that comes to mind is something Jim Cotter said, quoting Shakespeare, about being 'God's spies'.[8] I looked up this speech in *King Lear* and it's that lovely, sad yet so hopeful bit where Lear is finally redeemed from his power hunger and his intensely selfish politics and possessiveness and returns – if he'd ever been there before – to a gentle innocence. Real, rich, human communication, amused and ironic, sensitive, pleasurable in the restored, redeeming company of Cordelia so that they become 'God's spies' taking upon them 'the mystery

8. William Shakespeare, *King Lear*.

of things'. But of course he's frail and old and – worse – they're on their way to prison in defeat, and about to die. It's in that context that he sings this lyrical celebration of life and real human contact – detached from and amused by the politicking and power-mongering, preferring 'the mystery of things'. '. . . upon such sacrifices, my Cordelia', he says, 'the gods themselves throw incense'.

My prison is AIDS – I don't choose to go there but that doesn't mean I can't try to sing in this cage: I can try to take in 'the mystery of things' as if I were 'God's spy. . . .'

I notice now that as well as living and praying and singing Lear tells Cordelia that they'll also 'tell old tales'. . . .

A little later, struggling with the same question of living beyond dying, the journal goes on:

> It's so obvious really – we acknowledge that so many things that we polarise are not really opposites at all: black and white, subjective and objective, male and female. And the same surely is true of life and death. Not opposites but part of a single whole thing for which, in a sense, we have no name.

I have always been struck, ever since I read it at Cambridge, by a phrase of Professor Nicholas Lash: 'Death is the impenetrably dark face of coming alive.'[9] I don't think the stories – yet – have fully faced the sheer 'nothing' which is death, the impenetrable darkness. Perhaps it is glimpsed; in any case the struggle goes on.

More recently something else has happened. The phrase quoted above from Nicholas Lash occurs in an essay about death in his book *Theology on Dover Beach*.

9. Nicholas Lash, *Theology on Dover Beach* (Darton, Longman and Todd, 1979).

The essay emphasises how impossibly hard it is for us to think about life 'after death'. Since death ends our time-bound lives there can be no 'before' or 'after' and, in fact, no meaningful talk at all. I had felt this difficulty already and have continued to feel completely tongue-tied in speaking of 'life after death'. This can be a problem pastorally in the parish when people want to know what has 'happened to' the dead. I have found it hard to confirm ideas about 'being with Jesus', 'meeting again in heaven' and while I have declared in the creeds what the Church says about the 'resurrection of the body' I have not really known what I mean by that! I have not, however, been able to say either that there is nothing; it has simply been a total inability to be articulate about something for which there can be no language.

And yet now . . . now I find myself deeply moved by the powerful sense of longing in some of the great mediaeval hymns of heaven: the hymns of St Bernard like 'Jerusalem the Golden' or this from the fifteenth century:

> O how glorious and resplendent,
> Fragile body, shalt thou be,
> When endued with so much beauty,
> Full of health and strong and free,
> Full of vigour, full of pleasure
> That shall last eternally!

Of course it has a special poignancy now to believe in such a 'resurrection body' – so much beauty, full of vigour . . . but I feel as if I can think of this too as 'metaphor', as 'story', rather than taking it literally. It is metaphor to express what we have no words for, another kind of beautiful, hopeful story.

More recently I have felt the same sharp, poignant

longing in Negro Spirituals, no doubt evoked by the harshness of their oppression too: 'A band of angels coming after me, Coming for to carry me home.' When I have no energy, when I am drained by the struggle to carry on living as normally as possible, when it's hard to read, to think, to pray I share the longing in those songs, that music, that story-shaping for the angel chariot, coming over Jordan.

I suppose that all of this might still be a huge self-deception and escapism. We are always very ready to cloak the emptiness and try to find words – stories – to avoid the yawning vacuum of death. It is necessary to keep asking if that is what I am doing but at the moment I do not feel self-deluded in that way.

What I have come to feel I can affirm at the heart of the contemplation of dying, death and 'after' is, if I believe that life is lived within the love of God – and I believe that more and more – then death too is in that love. To die (and here immediately come the metaphors again) is to go deeper into that love, never further away, to be more fully embraced . . . but, again, what precisely that means I do not know. I feel like a little stream or river that makes its way to the ocean – it returns to the vast ocean of life and God, it becomes undifferentiated, absorbed in that sea of love.

In this context I have always been moved, though still without full understanding, by the words of St Paul: 'Here we sigh that what is mortal may be swallowed up by life.'

I do not somehow feel that sense of 'being absorbed', of being 'swallowed up', as frightening or threatening. Although I am unlikely to live my 'allotted span' I am not bitter or afraid. I don't exactly know why but a little phrase that occurs repeatedly in the journals – and in my head – is 'it doesn't matter'. My little life returns to the flow of things, there is something falsely assertive and possessive about the frantic desire to 'make my mark'.

I have been part – a tiny part – of the movement of life, it flows on. Blaise Pascal contemplated the 'eternal silence' of the universe's vast spaces and was afraid but for some reason I find it comforting to be so tiny, not to matter, to be absorbed into the waiting ocean. In this way I can let go and be ready. I am getting nearer to leaving nothing of which I am afraid.

But there is fear still, some of the stories witness to the groanings and the terrors that remain. Like anyone I am afraid of pain, I am afraid of blindness and dementia. At the moment I need nutrition to be fed directly into my bloodstream as my digestive system no longer works, I need daily treatment to prevent the partial loss of sight in my right eye deteriorating into blindness. There are the minor indignities of diarrhoea and sickness and sheer weariness which I hate, and I am frightened of them worsening. I am frightened of being dependent, needing to be 'looked after', I have been so self-sufficient, so independent. There are more nameless fears, the yawning gap inside in the night sometimes, the dreams, a sense of hopelessness, depression. And so I struggle not to give in to fear, to its isolation and loneliness, to its prejudices and selfishness.

I have not had to feel alone. The centre and focus for me of a sense of 'belonging', of not being on my own in this, has been the Eucharist. And the Eucharist, as well as some of the Healing Services we have had, has been the place for some of the stories. The Eucharist itself is a form of story, a web of metaphors, but for me so dense it cannot be fully comprehended. It links together so many essential themes – community and communication, self-examination and development, healing and release, peace and longing, grace and love. . . . One of the deepest moments in it for me is the Fraction when, in the breaking of the bread, the presence of Christ is shared among us, healing is offered but only through brokenness, life through sacrifice, when we begin again the story of the one Body by entering into its – his – death and only that way finding life. My life is framed, then, here by the Paschal Mystery, by the story of the dying and rising of Christ. It does not so much provide a way of understanding death but simply of facing it, taking it fully into account, of swallowing it in life. In all of this there has been a return of some of the simplicity and straightforwardness of my childhood attempts to 'follow Jesus'. I can hear his parables more freshly, accompany him in Holy Week, even love the Psalter with him as a deeply personal prayer book. (Like Psalm 91: 'you shall not be afraid of any terror by night . . . of the pestilence that walks about in darkness, or the plague that destroys at noonday.' All the ironies and the comfort.) Above all perhaps the celebration of the Great Easter Vigil, the waiting in the dark and the hoping, the knowing what would come with the dawn. This is a well of healing for me where there is no room for fear, love crowds it out.

And it has been a place for my stories too. This is part of the interwoven development referred to earlier. The stories emerged in me along with the desire to share the experience of illness, to find a way of speaking of it, even as it progressed and as I was able to turn and face it more fully. Many of the stories are only distantly related to my personal experience but they are related and here I could let something of the heart below the mind reach for the surface. I could hope too that there might be echoes for others. I have not felt that I am on a lonely journey now

29

away from everyone else but that still our experience is shared and that we all are 'living in the face of dying'.

My 'letting go' then, mentioned earlier, is not for growing isolation, a solitary, private descent into dying, but a detachment that actually makes a commitment to human life in its integrity and diversity more intense and fierce. A greater love of justice and mutual trust and human hope, a yearning for healing, grows and burns as long as it can. Simone Weil in her book *Waiting on God* says that the quest for the Holy Grail is won by the knight who comes to the Wounded King and asks: 'What are you going through?'[10]

That desire to understand, to identify with the world's pain, to reach its wounds, is made strangely easier by being wounded oneself. There is a solidarity, an understanding that I have personally felt in the parish and beyond and if the fears that would turn the affliction merely inwards in a self-destructive way can be resisted, then mysteriously the wounds contribute to a possibility of healing, for me and for others too. Somehow the 'stories' are all part of that.

During the media attention focussed on this 'vicar with AIDS', at the beginning of 1995 I was asked to give an interview for Radio Scotland for which I had to go to the Radio Sheffield studio. They put me in a small padded studio cubicle on my own with headphones and a microphone, the interviewer was a disembodied voice, I talked to the wall. She asked me at the end of the interview how I would like to be remembered, what I wanted people to say about me. I said that I hoped people would be able to say, at last, that I had some integrity.

Facing the wall, confronting my brick wall, has been

10. Simone Weil, *Waiting on God* (Routledge Kegan Paul, 1951).

about trying to find that integrity. That has meant facing myself and facing others, being as honest as I can be, and that has meant telling 'stories'. So I could begin to answer the questions that otherwise left me speechless, so I could begin to communicate out of affliction and into a kind of healing. So I could live into – even in the face of dying – something like integrity.

Part II

STORIES IN CONTEXT

ALL SHALL BE WELL

ON MY bedroom wall is a framed postcard. The caption says: 'Everything is going to be all right'. Perhaps it sounds like a cliché, but for me, seeing it there every day, it has become something of a motto, a feeling I carry around with me, a more deeply-seated conviction. How, you may say, can that be in any sense meaningful since you're living with AIDS? A good question.

I made a programme with the BBC in the *Everyman* series about living with AIDS and at the same time continuing to be a parish priest. The programme inevitably approached all the issues raised in this situation. The issue of coping in the parish and in the wider Church (and personally) with this feared condition. The issue of homosexuality and the Church, homosexuality and the priesthood. The issue of trying to continue to minister out of infirmity. And many other issues. Why, you may ask, so deliberately raise all these issues? Why disturb the peace of the Church yet again over sex and sexuality? Why risk the peace of your family and friends – your own peace?

For a long time living with an HIV Positive diagnosis was for me a brick wall, a desert, a wilderness that seemed spiritually unapproachable. I didn't know what to do with it. It stayed in me as an unexplored, uncomfortable secret. But secrecy is tiring, concealment – and what amounted sometimes to deception – is a huge extra burden alongside the virus itself. As symptoms began to develop I began to divulge my 'secret' and at the same time I seemed to be able also to face the brick wall, to enter the desert and begin tentatively to explore the wilderness. I don't quite understand the connection between opening up to others and something opening up within, but it was – is – real for me. I remain an 'inward' kind of person and yet I find myself being increasingly public about a profoundly personal situation. You may be asking why. Why make a film? Why talk to the press?

There are of course so many reasons, including those I can't articulate, but here are some: I wanted to say that you *can* live with AIDS. I wanted to say this both to others who are HIV Positive but also to the rest of the world that assumes it's HIV Negative. My immunity is seriously compromised, I am vulnerable to infections. I live with an inability to take nutrition from food so I'm 'fed' intravenously through the night. I live with a virus affecting my eyesight which also requires daily intravenous drug treatment. I live with other limitations and minor infections as well as the side effects of drugs but I am still living and working too. More than anything else, in the media attention I've resented the description of me as a 'dying man'. Of course I know that I'm very vulnerable to new infections that could change everything, but in this moment – the one in which I live – I am living, awake, aware and alive.

So I wanted to say that it need not take over your life. It's there always of course, the shadow at your shoulder, but that somehow just invites defiance, as so many others have demonstrated. We are not victims, we can keep it in its place. There are other things I want to do while I can – other things in which AIDS is irrelevant. It can be kept in its place while living and creating and growing goes on. The shadow is real enough in the parish, for instance, but our ordinary life goes on. We are living with it not under it, still less dying from it. There are those of course who want to make me a victim – because of their own fears or even because they can only care for others by making them into victims – but I, along with many others in this condition and with similar life-threatening illnesses – I intend to hold my head up, to stand upright and live.

And I also wanted to speak out openly in celebration of the support of the local church: our own parish and other local Christians too. So much support, so much practical help, so much prayer. I live with the irony, as so many do, of an openness of love and affection stirred in me, in others, by the prospect of dying.

But I did want also – less consciously perhaps, less clearly – to press the issues in the wider Church too. AIDS, sexuality, homosexuality . . . at heart I'm only ever a reluctant campaigner and yet there is something too important, too central, here to suppress. Deliberately or not, the Church induces so much prejudice and fear and guilt in this area. Deep-seated guilt in those who happen to be 'different', a lurking guilt, destructive and deathly, in those who happen to be ill with this condition. Isn't there enough to carry without this too? People with AIDS – and also gay people generally – need so much extra courage and defiance and dignity and integrity to throw off this demeaning guilt in the face of the Church. But they do it – and that needs celebrating too.

And maybe most of all, but somehow hardest to find words for, I wanted to say something about living in the face of dying. It is of course what we are all doing but those who live with terminal illness are forced to have, are given perhaps, a special vantage point, maybe even a vocation to live directly in the face of dying and speak – if they can – from there. Of course I am afraid. I'm afraid of pain, of weakness and disability. I'm afraid especially of dementia – I live so much in my mind, how could I live without it? I'm afraid of all the little failures and indignities that go with this condition, the lack of agility, the inability to run, to dance. . . . I'm afraid, hate the idea, of being dependent, a burden. So I'm afraid of being mortal – a fragile 'living creature'. W. H. Auden's words go round in my head:

> . . . in my arms till break of day
> Let the living creature lie
> Mortal, guilty, but to me
> The entirely beautiful.

It's the last line that keeps me alive. Yes, I'm afraid. I'm mortal, I share in the guilt of the world, but living in the face of dying has transformed the world as well. I see that it is – we are – 'entirely beautiful', however fragile. Colours are more intensely real (yellow has simply come alive for me). The simplest things are so beautiful. People are beautiful.

And God doesn't go away – not for me – but draws closer and closer. In Passiontide this year I found myself accompanying Jesus in his pilgrimage towards dying more intensely, more personally, than I have ever done and he was – is – accompanying me. At the time I was in hospital for a blood transfusion . . . the resonances and ironies only grow stronger. And at the heart of this intensity of living for me is the Eucharist, receiving it, presiding at it. 'The body of Christ', 'the blood of Christ' – the words reverberate in me ever deeper and deeper down. All the implications of being part – organically integrated into – the body of Christ become more and more powerfully significant. In that body, in all its manifestations, with my virus, is where I am alive.

Before I was instituted as rector in Dinnington, I made a retreat which included a visit to what, for me, is one of the holiest places in England: the shrine of St Cuthbert in Durham Cathedral. As I sat there in the silence I heard, felt, a message that there was nothing to be afraid of. It was a deep reassurance. I applied it then of course to the institution and my first living. It did apply to that. But when I got home I found waiting for me the letter which urged me to contact the hospital which led to my positive diagnosis. And now of course I hear the message in this situation too. 'There is nothing to be afraid of.'

I don't know where courage comes from, I don't know why some seem to have it (like Dennis Potter in his extra-ordinary last interview who said he hadn't had a moment's terror in his illness) and others don't. It is what I pray for. The Breton fisherman's prayer has become one of my favourites, not least for its brevity: 'Help me God, the sea is so vast, my boat is so small.'

I feel like a boat in dock, being built, repaired. The tide is slowly coming in. . . . One by one the props are knocked away, sometimes more than one at once. . . . I rock, uncertain, unsteady. It feels destructive, deeply threatening, unstable, unbalancing. . . . But the tide is swirling in and I shall discover that the props have to go if I'm going into that great swelling ocean in my little boat, into the ocean that I'm made for. . . .

'Everything is going to be all right'. One of the modern versions uses that phrase to translate Mother Julian's 'All shall be well . . .' in her *Revelations*. I am praying for the courage to believe it and to live it.

'Sin is behovely but all shall be well and all shall be well and all manner of thing shall be well.'

The Desert

He was exhausted. He had trudged for hours and for miles down the long, long valley as it steadily widened. He had thought he might come to a lake but the stream had barely widened and now it trickled off towards the east and before him to the south was desert, breathtaking desert. He sat down beside a little tree at the side of the stream and looked, breathless. He was breathless because of the journey and his heavy load, he was breathless because of the hot sun high in the sky but he was breathless too because of the vast endless emptiness before him.

The sky was empty, the horizon was empty and all the space before him was a bleak, muddy-coloured emptiness. All the world seemed empty – not a sound, not a movement – beyond the stream – all perfectly still. He sat and gazed, behind him the valley he had struggled down – lusher higher up, drier and sparse as it reached the edge of the wilderness. As he gazed the desert was daunting, forbidding, frightening but the more he contemplated it, the more it intrigued and held him – the sheer emptiness, the vast space, unexplored, untouched, unattempted.

He sat and stared for many hours and slowly the sun changed and the light faded, the wilderness changed colour and he shook himself as if waking up. As night fell he began to set up his tent and he looked around to plan his next day's journey. Along the stream perhaps?

But over and again, even in the darkness, he found himself gazing into the bleak wilderness: an echoing blackness now, unending and borderless.

As he lay down a bird began to sing, the first solitary sound he had heard. Its song, as he listened, was of the wilderness, sad, beautiful, spacious, haunting . . . as sleep came he knew with certainty where his exploration lay, across the wilderness, to its end.

The bird woke him in the morning with the rising of the sun. It was singing still for him of all that space to explore. But there was another edge to its melody, an echo he didn't understand, different from the night before. But he whistled what he could pick up of the tune and folded his tent and loaded his bag and, before the sun was much higher, he had set off, over the stream, and into the forbidding landscape.

He trudged for hours, whistling at first, but soon too tired. The sun grew hotter and the landscape more bleak and dry, more abandoned and oppressive. The pack on his back was heavier and heavier and all around was blank, unresponding emptiness. Sweat poured into his eyes and he determined to sit and rest – if only he could find something to rest against in this emptiness . . .

And there it was, with a groan he realised, the stream and the tree he had set out from. He had trudged a great circle and was back where he had begun.

He discarded his load and sat down against the tree and, as the sun reached its height, contemplated again that vast emptiness, staring hour after hour.

As night began to fall again the bird began to sing again. As he listened the other echoes were in its song once more. He listened, his head on one side, carefully to all the melody and its echoes and began to hear the song of the wilderness. He nodded slowly and smiled –

41

and this night, as darkness fell, he didn't erect his tent but went on sitting in the expanding gloom.

In the silence of the dead of night, when all was an even darkness everywhere, the bird sang again, a new song. She sang of the morning when the sun would rise on the wilderness and by the stream would be a folded tent and a huge bag and a neat heap of a man's clothes. There would be a footprint in the mud of the stream and a fast-disappearing track out into the wilderness. And on the deserted horizon so far, far away there would be, dim but clear in the still air, a man's voice, a traveller's voice, answering her song, singing alone, lightly, a song of the desert, further and further off, without a word, fainter and fainter, lost now, far, far away.

The Boat in Dock

She groaned a little. The repairs had taken a long time but were nearly finished – her little cry was not so much of pain as of longing, inarticulate longing. The workers tapped her sides, running hands over smooth wood, checking the curves of the hull and the prow. The damage had been serious, deep holes and long splits in weak timbers. She had been out of the water for weeks, high and dry on the lightly creaking props. A ship-wright's plane ran along a final smoothed plank of her little deck. She had felt exposed, naked, as they'd cut away her damaged parts – at night the dry dock was quiet, lonely. She felt isolated, vulnerable, even afraid. Far away, it seemed, there was the dim roar of the ocean. It stirred something deep within her but the stirrings were smothered by the fierce sharp reality of the knocking hammers, the skimming planes, the sharp nails. The shipwright ran his hand again all along her length. It was as if she shuddered a little, shivering as she waited, he thought. His skilful eyes checked over her repairs, nodding, tapping the shining new wood in the raw spaces cut deep from the old rottenness. She was tender still and seemed to shiver again. He patted her lovingly again and turned listening to the distant sea, to the sound of the tide. He nodded with satisfaction and – still nodding – left her waiting, aching, hoping.

So they came. The workers raised the great sledge-hammers and with a single blow knocked away the props, two at once, so that she lurched and tipped, frightened and confused. 'Careful!' yelled the shipwright, his hands on the lurching boat, his eye still checking the truth of her lines, his ear catching, above the din of knocking, the nearer surging of the sea, the tide rolling in. Lurching still she heard it too – nearer, an almost forgotten roar. She braced herself for the other props to be knocked away – she knew they had to go, she knew how she would tip and lurch again, she braced herself and felt the longing surge within her, her timbers aching now for their destiny. She thrilled in a little shiver for the sound of the coming ocean. It was what she was made for. She seemed to reach out in her longing, out to meet the sea. And the hammers swung towards the last of the props.

THE TRANSFORMING OF WOUNDS

I AM WRITING this from hospital – a place for the wounded, a place, one hopes, for the healing of wounds, at least, sometimes. I'm here for tests and treatment as a result of one of my 'wounds' – the AIDS condition. We are all wounded – to be human is to have wounds and I want to reflect on three ways in which I have seen myself as wounded and what that has meant – and means – about the God I believe in.

AIDS is obviously one of those wounds and I shall come back to that. Related to that I have seen my homosexuality as a wound and, again partly as a result of that, I have seen my whole self as 'wounded'. I grew up within a conservative evangelical religious culture that reflected and only slightly exaggerated the prevailing attitudes of a wider social society – everything told me I was flawed, misshapen, wounded. I had not chosen to be like this, the wound was part of me, so the flaw seemed deep but, equally, could not be ignored. It was not – is not – the most important thing about me but it is nevertheless *an* important thing and central. So, slowly, over the years, holding those two things together before God as I must do if God was to have all of me – holding both the importance of this 'flaw' *and* its given-ness, its rootedness in me, letting God's light shine, I began to see it was not a wound at all but a gift, not a flaw but a grace. I'm not going to enter here into arguments about homo-sexuality, what I am saying is that for me before God this

45

was the change that slowly occurred. It contributed, of course, to the same more general experience about my whole self – and it *gained* from what I increasingly saw about myself before God. A quiet – even shy – personality was not a flaw but a grace, my 'inferiority', inwardness that could seem like self-sufficiency, was not a wound but a gift, a gift to be developed and explored and used. My reticence was not a mistake to be corrected but part of God in me to be enjoyed and celebrated. (Quietly, of course. . . .) And so then, too, with that other wound transformed, my sexual identity – part of God in me to be enjoyed and celebrated so that the world could see the rich diversity of the divine gifts, the scope of the love that changes wounds into gifts. . . .

That transformation was not an easy process but the idea of seeing the 'wound' of AIDS as a gift looked impossibly hard. I'm not one of those who, living with AIDS, have come to say that 'it was the best thing that happened to me' (for the changed priorities in living, the new perceptions, the love that is often offered). There *are* real wounds, profound sufferings that are not to be transformed into gifts so easily and yet I do know that here too for me life does become vivid, sharp and intense, there *is* something of grace about having to live in the face of death.

Let me turn from the wounds to the Transformer of Wounds. This is a God who not only heals but heals by changing what seemed to be ailment into a place of gifts and graces and presences. What kind of a God is this?

The longer I live before God the more difficult it seems to begin to talk precisely about what I believe. It's the difficulty of being *inside* your subject. . . . It's the difficulty of the journey in which the God you follow keeps changing form – growing so large, disappearing, hiding. . . .

This is, of course, not God's problem but mine – the follower's perception. So the God I follow is a mysterious intimacy (but can you *follow* an intimacy?); a ground for joy; a depth deeper than I can go, out of reach and yet so desirable. And God is – again – out of reach not because *God* runs away but because I look in the wrong place, searching the universe when I should look deeper *within* (which turns out to be searching the universe anyway . . .). It sometimes seems like a little child playing hide and seek, continually emerging in delight from unexpected places, the hiding places given away only by the laughter of the child (*God* of course is the child, not me . . .).

'The best journey to make', says the poet R. S. Thomas in one of my favourite quotations, 'is inward.'

So God, for me, has gone from outside to inward, from 'mine' – a possession, a private concern – to something uncontrollable, wild even, but always beautiful; from judge, moral arbiter to someone almost embarrassingly undiscriminating in the readiness of welcome.

I feel as if I have learnt most of this in the liturgy. The liturgy is a 'black hole' full of the most dense meanings and implications but my journey – if anywhere – has been along its edges. It matters to me intensely, of course, to be able to preside at it but, in fact, it has taught me precisely that its dense mysteries are for everyone equally or they're for no one. So it was the transforming of Christ's wounds into our healing food that helped to give me acceptance. Acceptance as a first characteristic of God, acceptance as written right through the divine nature, acceptance that included self-acceptance. So the liturgy taught me 'body' too – the interchangeable body of Christ on the altar and the body of Christ in the pews, the one always making the other – and vice versa. And, in truth *my* body – organically linked to that glorious body (both of them, all of them . . .) – acceptable, even beautiful, a temple, a shrine, even now. . . . And the liturgy taught me justice – its radical equality, its affirming of integrity in each and every one of us, its unashamed love of truth and trust, goodness and honesty. And it taught me hope. . . .

What hope do I live with? Can you have hope and live with AIDS? All kinds of hopes are possible, in fact, but what of 'after death'? It feels like the wrong question – as with God, so here, I become *more* inarticulate. Except that it has to be deeper into love, into that welcome and acceptance – it feels like an ocean of it – love – waiting, its abysses bottomless, but clear and warm. . . .

To my own surprise – and no doubt for others too – I am rarely depressed (despite the ending of the *Everyman* film). I find myself with a sort of contentment, with a quiet joy, with a sense of a place in the universe – a *tiny* place in so vast a beauty, a quite insignificant place and yet a real little place that was – is – mine. Maybe all this is the result of a massive self-deception but it doesn't feel like that, it is not what my attempts at careful self-examination show me. It feels like a real kind of growing – it feels like a real preparation. . . .

The Gifts

He was cold even though the fire was lit and glowing in
the hearth. He curled up more tightly in the chair, feeling sorry for himself. The house was empty and quiet.
It felt to him as if it had always been like that. Empty
and quiet – and lonely. He sighed and curled up more
tightly still.

Suddenly there was a loud knocking at the door. He
was shocked, surprised, frightened: who could it be? No
one knocked on his door, no one came, who could it
be? He sat still and motionless, perhaps they would go
away. . . . With a shiver he heard the knock again –
louder, longer, more enthusiastic. Slowly he uncurled
and got up and hobbled into the hall. He could see
nothing through the little frosted window of the door
and nothing through the keyhole. He stood still and
silent hoping they hadn't heard him. He gave a little
moan as the knocking came again on the door. They
were not going to go away, he would have to answer the
door. He straightened up to look at the bolts and the key
and the chain on the door, he knew they would be
stiff . . . he sighed, he could just shout Go Away! he
thought but they were knocking again – loud, insistent,
demanding. He reached for the bottom bolt, muttering
'Just a minute, just a minute . . .'. It took an effort but
with a thud it flew back and he stood up to get his breath.
He tugged at the top bolt, stiffer still, but soon it gave
and he paused again for breath. They were knocking

again, harder and harder. Who could it be? With both hands he turned the key, took a deep breath, made sure the chain was secure and opened the door a few creaking inches.

'They're for you!'

A little girl stood there, beaming, shuffling in excitement and her arms were full to overflowing with brightly coloured parcels. One hand was stuck out from beneath the tottering pile, ready to knock on the door again.

'They're for you!' she beamed again, dropping a few.

He was dazzled, shocked, frightened, peering through the crack in the door.

'Who are you?' he rasped. 'I don't know you, I don't know any children, go away.'

'But they're for you', she insisted, pushing the glowing gifts towards him. He hid behind the door.

'They can't be for me, nobody gives me presents, I don't deserve presents, you've got the wrong man, not me. . . .' He peered out again and she was still standing there, laughing and juggling all the parcels.

'No, but they're for you!' she said again.

'Go away!' he croaked, suddenly angry and frightened and he slammed the door, shuffling as fast as he could to get away as far as he could – into the kitchen. She was knocking again, as loud as ever, and he noticed that one bright red and silvery parcel had fallen over the threshold before he managed to shut the door. He shivered, puzzled, frightened. 'Nobody visits me', he said, 'nobody gives gifts to me.'

The knocking had stopped, his breathing began to slow again. He sighed. They did look wonderful those presents. . . .

He let out a cry of shock as suddenly the thunderous

knocking was right beside him at the back door. He could see the little girl's shape through the glass, he could hear her laughter, he could see the huge pile of gifts, bigger than ever, he was sure.

'Go away!' he yelled. In a burst of energy he threw open the door, 'Go away! I don't get presents!' he yelled.

'They're all for you!' she said, juggling them, dropping them on the mat, staggering under the size and weight and shape of them all.

'No!' he cried and tried to slam the door but some parcels got in the way and as he fled for the sitting-room he saw her head come smiling round the doorframe.

He leaned against the wall, breathing hard. He could hear her arranging the gifts in the kitchen, calling to him. 'They're all yours', she kept saying, 'I want to give them to you, please accept them, I really want you to have them all. . . .'

With a long moan he looked round the door into the kitchen. Perhaps I can just get an explanation, he thought. He picked up a beautifully-wrapped parcel lying at his feet as he stepped into the kitchen and held it. She was giggling and shuffling from one foot to the other. The kitchen around her was overflowing with the shining gifts. She spread out her hands:

'They're all for you', she smiled. 'Every single one. And please can I help you open them?'

The Lake Transformed

She sat in her usual place on the great stone at the water's edge and looked around. It didn't matter how many times she came here she never failed to give a little shiver of delight when she first sat down. She had started coming now very early in the day, before there were too many people about, while the water was still smooth and undisturbed, while the silence still hung over the lake and shore.

It was beautiful. The grass and wild flowers waved down to the edge of the lapping blue water. Further back the trees spread out along the path, with smaller new trees and bushes planted between the bigger trees – shades of green and brown in the breezes, spring colours and spring fragrances. She took a deep contented breath, looking out across the lake. It was beautiful. She could just see the other side of the water and in it, all across reflected, the trees and the clouds and morning blue of the sky. She listened carefully, no, she could hear nothing at all . . . except the gentle murmur of the water, the stirring of the breeze and the occasional 'ploop' of a fish.

And now her mind went back to the first time she had sat on this stone. She shivered again but this time with distaste. The stale stagnant smell had been the overwhelming thing, the grey scum on the thick polluted water, the rubbish and the hopeless ugliness.

She had just moved to a house nearby and been astonished to discover the deserted, rubbish-filled lake hiding in amongst sad trees. It was silted up, lifeless and polluted, grey and stinking of decay. As she perched on the stone she could see a supermarket trolley sticking out of the oozing mud, a car's exhaust pipe stuck up into the air further out in the water, a broken tree sprawled at the water's edge full of litter and dirt.

A wave of despair washed over her then as she sat there in the twilight surrounded by decay and ugliness and pollution. She shook her head, hating it, sad but unable to drag herself away. As she sat there it grew darker still and she began to be frightened by the loneliness of the place and its abandonment. At last she stood up to go. As she did so the full moon came into view and its light flickered across the lake. With a little gasp she saw the scene transfigured – it was bathed in light, beautiful, tranquil, the old metal shone, the water gleamed. There was a hint of heaven in the shining of the moon. The moon went in again but she stood transfixed.

'No', she said aloud, 'it doesn't have to be like this.' She could change it, save the lake from silting up, make it beautiful.

The very next day she strode down to the lake. She didn't give herself time at first to see the daunting scale of the mess, she began collecting rubbish and digging away at the edges. With weary arms though she began to see how big a job it was – desperately big, overwhelming.

Then she noticed someone sitting on her stone – a 'bag lady', scruffy, bent, staring at her.

'You'll never do it on your own, love', said the bag lady. 'You need some help.'

With that she got up and waded into the water to drag the supermarket trolley to the shore. They worked together for a while but two didn't make much difference either. Then she noticed a small group of children were watching them. Before she could say anything the bag lady had beckoned them over and was busy assigning them jobs to do.

It took months – over a year – the group of children grew, other people came and helped, steadily everything changed. Every so often the bag lady nodded to her and said: 'You'd never have done it on your own, love.'

She smiled as the memories flooded back – all that hard work, all that near-despair when it seemed the water would never be clean, then the first fish, the first irises, the first heron. . . .

People were calling to her now as they passed by the lake on the way to work or school, or as they strolled at the water's edge. She recognised the people she had worked with – still worked with – for the lake. She stood up to go. She patted the shining edge of the supermarket trolley, now a gleaming flower basket by the big stone, she smiled to see the car exhaust standing by the lake turned into a tall light for the path, it stood over a neat bench made from the broken tree. She looked back over the lake and felt it alive, hopeful and beautiful. She headed for home. As she reached the path she met the bag lady and they greeted each other. The bag lady was pushing a shopping trolley she had rescued from the lake, now her faithful companion. They looked together back over the lake:

'You'd never have done it on your own,' said the bag lady, 'but it is beautiful. It really is.'

WHAT IS SPIRITUALITY?

ONCE UPON a time there was a saint, a holy woman, who lived upon the mountain and the people would go out to her from the village to take their concerns to her, to talk with her, to sit in silence with her and pray. The saint sat always on a box.

It was obviously important and precious and special to her. One day someone said to her: 'Tell us what is in the box.'

Touching it lovingly she said: 'It is a secret.'

The people went away but some were curious now about the box. The next day someone else asked, 'What is in the box?'

She said: 'It is a secret.'

Now the curiosity of many villagers was aroused and the next day many more were clamouring: 'Tell us what is in the box.'

She said, 'It is a secret.'

So they organised a delegation led by the parish priest and arriving next day, he said: 'Reverend sister, tell us what is in the box; why do you protect it so? What is it, your cherished secret? What is in the box?'

She said: 'It is a secret.'

They drifted away frustrated and even more curious.

The next day the saint looked round on the assembled villagers and saw that they were still curious, still asking, 'What is in the box?'

Quietly she stood up and lifted the lid. The box was empty.

Grumbling and complaining and puzzled, the villagers drifted away. But a few remained. The saint sat down on the ground with the silent villagers around the open box and together they contemplated the Secret of the Box.

❖

What is spirituality?

First of all a warning. I once received a postcard from my younger sister. She has a talent for deflating my ego-balloons, and in it was a 'Biff' card in a series called 'Adventures in Conversation'. Number 4 is called 'Dealing with the male ego' and it shows a classic young couple eating together. He is saying: 'I'd like to go on about myself at great length if that's okay.' And she says, 'That'd be fine, Ken, honestly . . . but I'm late for a rehearsal already. Incidentally, did you know you've got your elbow in your lasagne?'

Spirituality is not 'going on about myself at great length' but that is such a temptation and is all too clearly what we sometimes do mean by 'spirituality'. Perhaps if I had the courage I'd do what they did at a conference of hermits I heard about. At the opening session the convenor said, 'Brothers and sisters, before we begin let us lift up our hearts to God.' And so they sat in silence for five minutes. Five minutes became fifteen minutes and fifteen minutes an hour – three hours they silently lifted up their hearts to God. By way of preparation – but I haven't got the courage. . . .

'Going on about myself . . .' Whether we like it or not, we are in the territory here of the subjective. The dictionary tells me that the word 'spirituality' was not used in the way we use it until the sixteenth and seventeenth centuries. In the age of greater self-consciousness, with Descartes – 'I think therefore I am' – and Bunyan's pilgrimage in spirit without moving from his cell, so we needed a word for this personal spiritual capacity: spirituality. Which leads me to another warning. This is a quite incredibly personal area – not surprisingly. We are talking about the deepest and tenderest things. Have you ever tried recommending that book you love, the one you keep reading, the one that gave you so much, changed your life? You enthuse about it to someone and they come back with a puzzled, slightly embarrassed look and a shrug. 'Well, actually I didn't quite finish it . . .' they say, and their bookmark is still in at page six . . . and you feel crestfallen. It meant so much to you and touched them not at all.

In the end there are no maps and prescriptions, all you can do is help people have the courage to set off and go, all you can do is defer to, show reverence for, the mysterious individuality of another person as they set off, as they stride ahead of you in the far distance, as they move off in a completely unexpected direction. We have begun to acknowledge that there are all kinds of subtle variations in types of spirituality – of women and men, of young and old, of cultures, of sexual orientation. . . . There is quite enough space for all of it. When they asked Rubinstein if he believed in God he said, 'Oh no, I believe in something much bigger.' In a General Synod debate in 1986 the Bishop of Durham said: 'We are always trying to pin God down by getting it cut and dried and decisive. God is always wanting to set us free to share in the mystery.'

So all I can do here is start where I am. It's enormously difficult to piece it all together so what you will get is fragments, bits and pieces from which to construct something. 'Fragments to shore against my ruins', as Eliot put it in his *Waste Land*.

I shall start where I am and where I am is Australia . . . I've never been there, I have no Australian friends, I have seen *Neighbours* . . . but this began with a book: *Creation Spirituality and the Dreamtime*,[1] that mysterious, evocative, deep and magical other-world-in-this-world of the Aboriginal Australians. One of the essays in the book pointed out how European Australians cling to the fringes of the continent. All the major cities are on the coast, the interior is unexplored, the Outback is a frightening wilderness, to be left well alone. But still for the Aborigine, for 40,000 years and still now, it is home and dream time and precisely mapped and located by their lines of song, described by Bruce Chatwin in his entrancing book, *The Songlines*.

Did you hear the interior echoes and resonances in that? That vast unexplored interior, but the space that seems a wilderness – a wasteland – but can be a dream time, our clinging to the edge. . . .

What is spirituality? Someone said the psyche is a holy land, but first it's a wilderness, a place of fears, vast, empty, unexplored territory that is frightening. It is Australia.

A story. I belong to a group in our diocese called 'Compost Heap'. It's an experimental worship group and that obviously also means a 'spirituality exploring group'. You can no doubt work out the name – the old and dead going onto the heap to be reused for growth and beauty.

1. *Creation Spirituality and the Dreamtime*, Catherine Hammond (ed.) (Millennium Books, 1991).

I wanted to put together a liturgy for the group using what I've just said about Australia. I racked my brains to think of a concrete image we could use – in my sitting-room – to picture that wilderness, that empty, unexplored interior. I thought of rocks and sand and cactus, but it wasn't quite right. As I sat there thinking about this in my sitting-room, I slowly focussed on the room itself. In the centre of the room – before my very eyes, as it were, all the time – is a long, pine blanket chest used as a coffee table. Like everything else in my house it's covered with bits and pieces, but the box itself is quite empty, lift the lid and there's nothing there. So at the centre already was this image of the interior, the unexplored, the space, the empty, holy place. So in the liturgy we lifted the lid and talked about the unexplored, unbefriended interiors of our lives, so – in due course – we filled the box with coloured tissue for our prayers, so we shared milk and honey to make the land Holy and Promised instead of Waste and Wild.

While I was still thinking through all that, in preparation, I was rivetted to hear this poem 'The Arrival of the Bee Box', by Sylvia Plath read on the radio. I just caught it driving along in the car. We used it of course in the liturgy:

> I ordered this, this clean wood box
> Square as a chair and almost too heavy
>   to lift.
> I would say it was the coffin of a midget
> Or a square baby
> Were there not such a din in it.
>
> The box is locked, it is dangerous.
> I have to live with it overnight

And I can't keep away from it.
There are no windows, so I can't see what
   is in there.
There is only a little grid, no exit.

I put my eye to the grid.
It is dark, dark,
With the swarmy feeling of African hands
Minute and shrunk for export,
Black on black, angrily clambering.

How can I let them out?
It is the noise that appals me most of all.
The unintelligible syllables.
It is like a Roman mob,
Small, taken one by one, but my god, together!

I lay my ear to furious Latin.
I am not a Caesar.
I have simply ordered a box of maniacs.
They can be sent back.
They can die, I need feed them nothing, I am
   the owner.

I wonder how hungry they are.
I wonder if they would forget me
If I just undid the locks and stood back and
   turned into a tree.
There is the laburnum, its blond colonnades,
And the petticoats of the cherry.

They might ignore me immediately
In my moon suit and funeral veil.
I am no source of honey

So why should they turn on me?
Tomorrow I will be sweet God, I will set them
   free.

The box is only temporary.

Do you hear the echoes? What is spirituality? It's something to do with attempting to explore all this resonating
territory, taking the risk, setting out. Something to do
with the capacity in us to make that beginning – the need,
the desire, the unrefusable urge. . . . In the words of R. S.
Thomas:

> Enough we have been given wings
> and a needle in the mind
> to respond to his bleak north.
>
> There are times even at the Pole
> when he, too, pauses in his withdrawal
> so that it is light there all night long.

This need, this desire, this 'needle in the mind', is right
at the very heart of us, deep at my mysterious centre and
yet it's a deeply common, shared thing too. We are not
talking of self-centredness here ('going on about myself
at great length.') but its precise opposite.

Another story. Dinnington where I live is a small town
that still thinks it's a village. It was a pit village with all that
means. Last year they closed the pit, after 89 years. So we
had a service in the parish church to mark the closure –
the mayor came, the bishop came and the people came.

61

The church was packed. As I waited at the door for the service to begin I heard the whine of the pit buzzer that used to announce shift changes – as well as emergencies. Not used for years, they had 'rescued' it to announce this shift, this great change. It was a piece of nostalgia and a warning too.

The service began in the dark and the bell tolled 89 times for the passing of the colliery. Then in the darkness three children entered with miners' lamps, a procession of light, and using prayers from the new Advent book we blessed the light and prayed for the future. Children from the local school performed a 'chorus for coal', a miner and a miner's wife told their stories, we blessed a Union banner to keep in church, the bishop preached.

Then the climax. We had already planned to create in church a memorial to those who had died over the years in the colliery, this became a golden chance to present that project – a community arts' project with artists working with local people, drawing on their spirituality. It was due to fill the space of the huge, floor to ceiling western screen wall in the church. We invited the congregation to stand and literally look back, turning to the west. As they did so the lights were extinguished and spotlights lit up the silhouettes on the glass of the screen depicting miners and mining, lamps and the great wheel. . . . It was frankly a moment of awe and fascination, a lifting of spirit, a stirring of hearts. Afterwards and ever since, people could hardly find words to explain what had gone through their minds and hearts then: it is moving to hear it.

There is a spirituality of the community, a common search and a shared journey. We can neglect it but it is part of being human that there is this shared desire, a common holy place. Spirituality is not about individualism though some have gone off along that path. Not 'mine' but 'ours'. And here the Church herself offers us her Body as a place in which to work this out – the corporateness of this organism we are part of: not ever more esoteric and private self-indulgences but exploration tested against the Body, held within the community. For me experimental prayer and worship is not strictly 'alternative' to the life of the Church but always to be fed back in. Exploring spirituality shouldn't take us further and further away from the mainstream church, tiresome as it sometimes is, but should feed the life there and make it a better place for exploration and the search. Far from being scorned the traditional and regular prayers of the Church – and especially the Eucharist – are where we ought to expect to be fed for the journey, not least because they have fed so many others. 'Ah, the prayers of my Mother, the Church of England', said another of my heroes, the poet, George Herbert, 'no other prayers are equal to them!'

What is spirituality? The corporateness of the journey leads to another fragment, another thread. Spirituality is in danger of being the subtlest and most devious of the Thatcherite privatisations. I think we have let these things – justice and prayer, spirituality and politics – get impossibly separated. Ken Leech has written in *Review of Theology*: 'In the present climate might it be better to get away from this kind of language [of 'personal spirituality'] and speak instead of the struggle for justice which embraces both inward discipline and outward activity?'

That seems to me like an integration that is very far away from most of us, a continuity of the seeking for justice, inward and outward – but what a thought! Charles Peguy said: 'Everything important begins in mysticism and ends in politics': the same continuity surely, a continuity we see in Jesus, but how often elsewhere?

What is spirituality? It surely only has a depth that is continuous with the rest of our lives if it reckons with, confronts face to face, rather than trying to escape, oppression and prejudice, pain and violence, recession and poverty, failure, inadequacy, emptiness and fear. It is obvious enough when you think about it – but we don't – that for most people the most spiritual thing in their lives is their relationships. And that is precisely where we each meet the hell as well as the heaven of being a human being. I was profoundly struck when I first read them by these words of Bishop Peter Walker, formerly of Ely. I have been chewing at them ever since: 'The prayer problem is the problem of one's own unresolved personal violence and the will to dominate others.'[2]

To put it another way, no one can have inner without outer peace.

Another story. In Dinnington Church hall two men 'danced' for nearly an hour. They had been rehearsing in our hall so I asked them to give us a performance. 'Dance' is not the right word, 'physical theatre' they call it, a combination of acrobatics, mime, gymnastics, movement . . . it was the story of a relationship affected by AIDS. It was moving, affectionate, violent, erotic, touching, beautiful, strong, tender, dramatic, intense: it made you very aware of bodies, of wordlessness, of expression, and of our deep, deep reluctance to communicate. AIDS has surely become a powerful metaphor for all that we are most afraid of within, that darker interior, the fearful

2. Peter Walker, *Rediscovering the Middle Way* (London, Mowbray, 1988).

place. A metaphor for all that spirituality meets as it struggles to bring its justices together, inner and outer; a metaphor for our attitudes – our 'spiritual attitudes' to our bodies, our sexualities, our selves in their darkest aspect. Well, here was one way of confronting all that – if you couldn't actually dance, at least you could watch and be absorbed. The spirituality was in the creativity, the exploration here was in the wordless movement.

And the beauty in the dance was itself a brave confrontation of the darknesses, itself a working out of a spirituality. I hope I haven't so far given the impression that I think spirituality is all about fear and gloom and the dark, it isn't. Spirituality is our longing for beauty, too, and our capacity to recognise it, create it, let it burst and blossom within us in a way that makes us know – as nothing else is so sure – that the beauty is braver than the dark. 'Beauty will save the world', said Dostoevsky.

What these particular fragments coalesce into is the conviction, for me, that spirituality is not very much about intellect and cognition and the cerebral and it is very much about the imagination, metaphors and images, the symbol-recognising, symbol-making part of us. That weird way in which an image emerges in someone and is instantly recognised by someone else as the precise embodiment of their own experience too. I find myself close to saying that the imagination is the same thing as the soul, that questing, searching, longing, place in us that keeps making pictures, keeps trying images, that collects metaphors.

I'm not of course denigrating words. Goodness knows, I've used enough of them. They too can emerge from the imagination and feed back in, they need to be treated with reverence, we need, as Alan Ecclestone puts it, to be chaste in their presence. Some people think that language began as song, from the music in the voice emerged a meaning – spirituality might be a search for that original state, recapturing the melody, 'the first, fine, careless rapture'. But I think we can safely say we – and our culture – have overdone words. Let the imagination work elsewhere too. In the wordlessness of that dance was all the effort and urgency and energy of the metaphors of spirituality. What are the metaphors that resonate for you? The wilderness? The journey? The inner shrine? The river? The well? The sustaining food? The treasure? The Dance?

One other thing that the focus on symbol and metaphor as ways into the mystery leads onto is a rediscovery of body and earth. The metaphors from the material invite us to rediscover the material itself. 'Matter matters' for spirituality too: we are not trying to escape flesh but to enter into it. Pleasure – bodily pleasure – is spiritual, is spirituality, places are spirit, earth is spirit.

This seems to me to be an unerringly Christian way of spirituality, leading us right into the Incarnation, the divine affirmation of bodiliness as the venue for spirituality. T. S. Eliot in 'The Dry Salvages' from *Four Quartets* puts it like this, leading up to his one theological word in the whole deeply theological sequence:

> For most of us, there is only the unattended
> Moment, the moment in and out of time,
> The distraction fit, lost in a shaft of sunlight,
> The wild thyme unseen, or the winter lightning
> Or the waterfall, or music heard so deeply
> That it is not heard at all, but you are the music
> While the music lasts. These are only hints and
>   guesses,
> Hints followed by guesses; and the rest

Is prayer, observance, discipline, thought and
    action.
The hint half guessed, the gift half understood,
    is Incarnation.

The word – Incarnation – takes us back to Jesus. I mentioned him earlier. Perhaps, like me, he's been haunting you ever since. Talk of the spirituality of matter and flesh, of incarnation, of resonating metaphors, leads straight to him: seeds and sheltering trees, paths and doorways, fields, holes and treasures, secrets and cups of water, dough and bread, fish and wine, bread that is flesh, wine that is life, a death on a public gibbet that is a metaphor for the richest possible life, all that overflowing measure pressed down and poured out, rich and strange. . . . It's hard to grasp, mysteriously elusive but so powerful, so essential, so crucial.

What is spirituality? It's about following Jesus. I apologise to Evangelical companions for not mentioning that before but I'm trying to be honest about my fragments, my hints and guesses. It is following Jesus – which sounds easy but isn't. It would be easier if you could actually get near enough to him, but so much gets in the way.

'I understand Francis.' says the Irish poet Padraig Daly:

> all the stuff about the birds,
> Throwing his clothes at his father;
> the singing, praising heart . . .
> But I am blind still to the Jew
> my life traipses after.

But his metaphors are clearer – the songs of Jesus, if you

like. I can work with those, they echo and resonate, they illuminate my traipsing . . .

I must end. The final fragments need pushing into place. . . .

We need more imagination and less thinking.

We need more honesty and less dogmatism so that we are infinitely more tentative, more open and inclusive, less sure of ourselves.

We need – and here I begin to contradict myself – more of that effort and discipline that Leech referred to, seeking the inner justice that is one with the outer, more of Eliot's 'prayer, observance, discipline, thought and action'.

And we need much less effort too. Less of the frantic urgency, the near-hysterical intensity. Less of the endless talking in long addresses like this, more of the lifting up of our hearts in silence, less of the going on about myself, more of the relaxed listening and waiting and watching. 'Everything is going to be all right' as Mother Julian reminds us.

To put it another way, in the words of my favourite Zen saying:

> Sitting quietly, doing nothing, Spring comes and the grass grows by itself.

The Coracle

The lake was perfectly still as he sat among the tough springy grass on its shore. It was so still in the early morning light that every so often he reached down to flick his fingers in the water to be sure it really was a lake and not just a mirror for the sky and its few clouds, for the circle of mountains with their gullies and distantly silent waterfalls, with their rich green forests. It was the untouched stillness of the very beginning of the day and his eyes swept back and forth across the expanse of water to take it all in. There was no wind – in fact, the only movement of the air was his breathing and it slowed to an easy rhythm as he sat and gazed.

He tried to make out the further shore but he couldn't – the lake was too big. The mountains beyond seemed very far away and he tried to imagine the far shore. As he looked with quiet intent ahead of him to that invisible edge he noticed a flickering dot on the curve of the mirror of the lake. He watched it very slowly grow larger, moving towards him. It was a boat. He leaned forward. A tiny boat, a coracle. He could see the flashes of the single oar now and the ripple of the disturbed water. It flashed and flickered round the gliding boat, catching that early light. And behind it the water slid slowly back into its smooth reflections. As the boat drew steadily nearer on its straight course he could see the rower. She stood in the middle of the little boat and she dug the oar rhythmically into the water on each side of the coracle. The boat never dipped, she never shifted but for the flow of the stooping, side to side, propelling the boat straight forward. And the water was with her, its ripples all part of her rhythm, even its reflections seemed to be helping her on. It was the holy woman. As the boat drew towards the shore he stood up – she seemed to have chosen to land precisely where he sat. He stepped back and the little boat seemed to shoot forward now until it bumped gently against the few pebbles and the springy grass. She stepped, sure-footed, onto the land and turned to draw the boat after her. He wondered whether to offer help but before he could move she had slotted the oar across the woven bottom of the coracle and in one gesture, as it seemed, she swung the boat up in a great curve and over her head and onto her back. And water of the lake seemed to follow as it shook from the interweaving of the boat out in a smooth parabola of crystal light around her. He greeted her – the holy woman standing with her boat nestling on her back.

'Where have you come from?' he asked, remembering the distant boat emerging into sight across the water.

'From the far shore', she said, 'where the rushes are tall in the clear water and herons stand among the reeds.'

'Why did you go there?' he asked.

She turned gracefully and looked back across the lake, still once again but brighter now as the day grew. And again the drops sparkled on the weaving of the boat on her back.

'I followed the moon in the night as it curved its way across the lake. I kept behind it so that the flashing of the oars never ruffled the circle of the moon. I followed to the far shore and waited. In the darkness the moon moved on over the mountains but I could not follow so I

70

waited. Nothing moved in the darkness except sometimes for the lapping of the lake against the boat but I
waited. And then the day began to grow and, when the
lapping of the lake caught the first of the light, when I
saw that the rushes are tall in the clear water and
herons stand among the reeds, then I waited no longer
and turned the boat to follow the growing of the day.'

As she turned back towards him the last flashing
drops from the coracle caught, cold on the back of his
hand. The lake was still. The holy woman strode quietly
away with her coracle. He stared at the smooth water
and looked slowly up towards the far distant mountains and the far hidden shore of the lake.

'Where the rushes are tall in the clear water', he said
to himself, 'and herons stand among the reeds.'

The Golden Cord

The Holy Woman was spinning.

A few villagers had climbed the hillside as usual to be with her and they sat on the ground outside her hut and she was spinning. She had never spun before and they looked at each other, interested.

The thread was fine and white as it passed through her fingers from the wheel, she was wrapped in concentration on it as the wheel turned, the wool shrank, the thread grew and grew.

After a while she paused at the spinning and began instead to twist the thread, weaving it, plaiting it, turning it this way and that so that it slowly thickened into a cord – thick and strong. Then from her pocket she fetched a fine golden thread, thin and light but so bright and glistening it was dazzling to look at and steadily she began to weave the fine golden thread into the thicker cord.

The villagers watched fascinated but the light was fading and although the Holy Woman seemed to want to go on spinning and plaiting and twisting the golden thread, they had to return to their homes in the village. As they descended the hill they looked back at her, the evening light catching the glint of the still weaving thread – and they sighed at the dark prospect of the gloomy little village with its troubles, its factions, its squabbling elders and its quarrelling families. By the time they reached the streets they could no longer even see the Holy Woman's hut, never mind the spinning. The mountains closed in, the sky was dark, the village seemed to rumble with dissent.

The next day the villagers climbed the hillside again to see the Holy Woman and there she was – spinning and weaving and twisting the golden thread. And now they sat down around her and gazed at the cord. It was long and thick and woven with an intricate pattern of delicate shapes and twisting curves, it was smooth and neat but detailed and elaborate as well – and through it all was woven, shining and fine, the golden thread. It twisted and hid and gleamed, it turned back on itself and sprang out in another delightful pattern and ran its way the length of the growing cord.

The word began to spread – this beautiful cord – and other villagers began to arrive and to sit in awe at the feet of the spinning, weaving Holy Woman. The cord grew and the villagers gathered and watched – it seemed now to twist and shimmer with rainbow colours along its length spun from the flashing fingers, it piled and stretched and coiled in heaps around the villagers and on she went, spinning and weaving and twisting.

By now the news had spread and all the villagers were coming up the hillside – even the elders were arriving and finally the Mayor. Awed, they sat with the others on the ground and watched the growing cord with the golden thread and its spangle of lights and its pattern of beautiful shapes and intertwined, twisting and delicate figures.

As the Mayor sat down and reverently touched the cord as it lay near him, the Holy Woman stopped her weaving and spinning and sighed. She stood up and together – villagers and Holy Woman – they stared at the glowing mass of gold-threaded cord, coiled and twist-

ing at their feet. Then she stooped and taking the end of
the cord she began to move among the villagers. And
she began to turn the soft, glistening cord around their
wrists and waists and ankles. Some of the villagers pro-
tested at first – they didn't want to be tied up, still less
to be attached to the particular people they were sitting
near. . . . But she went on looping and linking and tying
around the great circle of the villagers until the cord
wound its way through everyone linking around the
Mayor's wrists and ankles and then finally around
the Holy Woman's waist last of all.

The villagers were silent, astonished, they could think
of nothing to say but stared at the shimmering cord that
bound them all together.

Then she began to run – and the cord would not give
way or release them but lifted them, one by one, after
her so that they all – exclaiming and astonished but
laughing too – began to run after her, with her, attached
to her. And she ran straight up the mountainside –
through the trees, over the stream, through the scrambling rocks, up and breathlessly up the mountain with
all the village trailing and clambering and straggling
after her, but all on their way, all following, with her, up
and up. . . .

And as they ran and climbed the cord twisted and
glinted among them and held them together and shone
and lifted them after her – all the way up the mountain-
side.

And then they were at the top and the wind caught
them. They stood gasping together in a great circle on
the peak and the breeze lifted the cord and let it float
among them and the high sunlight caught the gold
thread so that it shimmered and gleamed and dazzled.
She looked around and the villagers, still linked to her,

74

looked around with her. They gazed at the endless vista of green and purple valleys, at the banks of distant clouds and the far, far horizons – they gazed at the tiny little village down below them and saw it, loved it and were ashamed of their quarrels. And they gazed again with her at the high sun as it shone everywhere and as it caught and ran along the length of their shimmering cord.

And as their breath returned and as they felt the wind on their faces, high up there with the sun, they nodded to each other and nodded to the Holy Woman and gently touched the cord.

THE BODY OF CHRIST

It comes to me vividly as I place a fragment of broken bread into your outstretched hands and say 'the body of Christ'. These are infected hands, fingers, doing the distributing – not contagious and yet infected with a life-threatening, a body-threatening virus. And what I place in your hands is, I say also, a broken, crumbling, fragmented body for you to share in. As you share in the wide-open brokenness of Christ's body, his blood, his heart, you share in my destruction too – and in my reconstruction, in my healing, because my body is healed, eased, soothed by knowing that you share my pain. One of the principle reasons that I am able to carry on entering into this repeated, ever-deepening mystery with you is precisely because you go on sharing it with me, helping me carry it, letting me help you carry all the fragmentation and brokenness of body and heart that you bring, hold out, offer in your reaching hands. It's an exchange of bodies within the body of Christ, through the body, the blood of Christ. And by it we are given the much-needed courage to enter more and more deeply into the agonising mystery of suffering in the bodies of all the world, in the body of creation.

This 'body language' goes deep in Christian spirituality for all the trouble Christians have had reconciling themselves to bodily, physical, sexual, 'contagious' existence. This sacramental insistence is emphatic – your body is part of you, my body is inescapably me, our bodies are

76

a lovely, precious, cherishable, pleasure-making, passion-bearing outwardness for our spirits, our souls, our hearts. And more – your body is part of me, my body touches you, if only my fingers on your palm with that broken body-fragment. We are in touch inside the body of Christ, that's what it's for. We are physically indispensable to each other – to each other's prayer, to each other's lives, to each other's souls.

The body of Christ carries our diseases for us – I carry your unease, your discomfort, your pain; you carry my weakness, my incapacities, my vulnerabilities. The body is infected so the Church – one body, one fragmented soul – has cancer, has heart disease, has AIDS.

Is there healing for this body? Yes, there is healing. It's precisely in the sharing of our broken bodies, in the exposed raw openness of our communion that the healing comes. Fresh, cool, gentle healing – the soothing of sores, the easing of aching wounds. Cherished bodies, a resurrected Body. The Body of Christ.

HEALING AND BAPTISM

HOLY WEEK reminds me of my baptism – of the actual physical event. I was baptised, aged 11, by full immersion. It was a pool of warm water at the front of our Baptist church, in the floor. Each candidate was helped down into the water, the water rising up you steadily as you descended each step. The minister took me by the hand and led me to the middle of the pool. It was up to my eleven-year-old chest. Then he took me by the hands and by the scruff of the neck and tipped me right back under the water with a great splash as he said, 'I baptise you. . . .' Then he lifted me up and I climbed the steps at the other side and paddled away to be dried. . . . I vividly remember the swirling water above my face as I was under the water – I've no idea why I kept my eyes open.

Each of the days of Holy Week is like one of the steps down into that pool: steadily we go down further with Jesus into total immersion in his death, to drown with him, down, step by step, until, in the words of the psalmist, 'the waters have risen even to my throat'. The reading from Isaiah and the reading from Hebrews are both about 'identification': the Servant, the High Priest, Jesus, who comes alongside us, to identify with us. We go with him, he goes with us, identifies with us. And we in turn identify with each other, we are immersed in each other.

It's what that woman was doing for Jesus – some sense of his destiny, his need, his burden overtook her so strongly that silently, prayerfully, she had to anoint him, to pour fragrant oil all over him, to hear a forward echo of his dying, to seal his consecrated purpose, to show she was with him, cared as deeply as she could.

The waters into which we descend in Holy Week are the waters of other people's sickness and pain, of our own too, they're the deep waters of sadness and loneliness and desperation, of mental illness and depression and fear, they are the drowning waters of dying, death, mourning: the fearfulness of life that is ending, a future that is unknown – hope seems to be lost.

Holy Week takes us down these steps – our own baptism into Christ is about going down there with him, with all his people, his body, identified with him – stronger than that, at one with him. In his last intense personal conversation with his friends, the night before he died, the Thursday night as John records it, Jesus talks of 'abiding' in him; he abides in us . . . he is our abode. More simply still, he keeps saying: 'I am in you, you are in me . . . as I am in the Father so I am in you – and – so you must be in each other' – like being in water together, up to our necks, over our heads.

These waters have steps up the other side too. Easter is as much as anything else about baptism – your immersion in Christ, into his body . . . your resurrection with him, with his body, all of us alive together in life at its fullest. You can't get there by walking round the pool: you have to go down, right down, under, till it swirls above your face, then . . . then and only then, through dripping hair and with streaming eyes, you can look for – we can look together for – the steps up the other side to life and freshness and healing.

Water is about drowning and terror and destruction, about cleansing and washing clean, but it's also about freshness and quenched thirst, refreshment and gentle pleasure, restored life and growth.

I have spent some time in a hydrotherapy pool. Deep, warm water – up to my throat – relaxing, refreshing, restoring. We end the session with ten or fifteen minutes of simply floating . . . lots of supporting floats, gentle music, and all that deep water holding you up. That's part of my vision of heaven – to float in warm, deep water, to angelic music. I said more than once in answering all the letters I had after the *Everyman* programme that it felt like floating on a deep warm sea of support, holding me up. That's what baptism leads us to – to create that deep sea of prayer and help and healing for each other, for the hurt and aching, for a thirsty, a dry and lonely world.

Rich and Strange

All the abysses of the ocean suddenly were clear.
Lapis lazuli, aquamarine and green;
blue of the planet's curves in space,
translucent as echoes
all the way down.

Sunlight filtered
but clarity was the sea's own rhythm of grace
for a moment mirrored in a thousand shimmering fish.

The slow swell rose from the solemn fathoms:
and fell – deep, open, endless –
to the ocean's lucid heart.
And, warm, silent, still,
the soul dived all the way down.

Diving

The waves broke on the golden sand of the bay, catching the bright sunlight. We looked at each other and smiled as we waded into the sea. Together we adjusted our breathing apparatus and dived through the next gentle wave under the surface of the water.

We were still in the shallows but it was already a new world. The sun was bright still above the green swirling roof over us but here there was no breeze and no sounds from the beach, only everywhere the sea. As the water settled round us from our dive we saw, just below us, the smooth curving sand of the sea bottom, the occasional seaweed or shell – and fish. . . . In every direction little fish swam and swirled in darting groups and little shoals, catching the light and as suddenly vanishing, quietly appearing from nowhere – a dazzle of bright colour – and then gone. We looked out, away from the bay, and saw the fading greenness of the deeper ocean endlessly stretching in every direction – silent, warm still, inviting. We looked at each other – level still, our feet kicking slowly – we peered through goggles, grinning – and my companion's eyes said: 'Deeper, deeper', so I nodded and together we began to move through the enfolding sea towards the deeper water.

The sea bottom began to fall away and the greenness of the water seemed to deepen. Fish still swarmed silently around us but now there were rocks with waving plants and sea creatures, fronds of lovely colour and shapes and channels in the rock inviting us to explore. We went deeper and felt the water cooler, the swirling surface and the light further away. But here now we noticed a different light, a swirling in the water with us, ahead of us and around us, touching us, catching brightly and then passing over our equipment, our hands and faces. We looked at each other. The light was in the currents, paler green, flashing blue, crystal and sharp then a fading glow everywhere. The plants seemed to reach for it and the fish to swim in tune with it, giving it a life and a shape. All ahead the water was deeper and deeper green, a vast wall of sea that was not a barrier but an invitation.

I looked at my companion, reaching for her hand, and mouthed to her, 'Deeper' . . . and together we slowly swam on and down.

The light in the water – spiralling and dancing – seemed to go ahead of us. It seemed to pause and wait for us, to look round and let us catch up then surge on, spiralling ahead. It would disappear and suddenly flash again as if it had taken a quick circle right around our slowly swimming progress and was ready again to swim with us, to swim ahead of us. As slowly we moved deeper in the silent ocean the light changed and seemed a more even greening glow, less flashing and spinning, more a shade of colour to the sea itself. Still shoals of little fish hung in its shimmer, it gently caught a rock and quietly lit up great waving plants.

For a moment it seemed to intensify, a bright sharpness in the water ahead. We glanced at each other but without mouthing words we knew the invitation to go deeper still. This was deeper than we had been before, out into darker green, beyond rocks and plants, to the edge of the steep shelving of the ocean floor. To the edge of the abyss.

We swam on, seeing the surfaces now just a distant glimmer, watching the sea-bed slope more steeply, but following the beckoning swirl of the light's invitation: deeper still, further down, searching the depths. We looked at each other and saw the awe and surprise and longing on each other's faces as slowly the ocean floor sank effortlessly away into invisible green depths, down sheer into the endlessly silent water. We could see nothing – but it was not the emptiness of fear or even of danger, it was the mystery of the deepest place, the smooth, resonant darkness of the Deep.

The light had not gone but danced above the abyss, appearing and disappearing, content with our gazing and pondering, as we trod the water. But still the invitation was to go deeper – led and held in our searching – and we looked at the ocean below us and we looked at each other, smiling, and we gazed again at the deep.

Part III
STORIES

Flower

'What have you got in your hand?' said her mother.

The little girl opened her hand and her mother stared. She could hardly see anything.

'I found it in the park', said the little girl, breathlessly.

'It's only a seed', said her mother, 'throw it away and wash your hands.'

'Oh, no', said the little girl, looking gently at the tiny fleck of brown in her palm. 'Oh, no, I'm going to plant it.'

'Please yourself', said her mother, 'but hurry up. Tea's ready.'

The little girl found a huge plant pot and filled it with rich brown earth from the garden. Reverently she pushed the tiny seed deep into the warm soil. Her mother watched her and laughed.

'Now wash your hands', she said, making a mental note to tip the soil back in the garden soon.

But after tea she found the little girl sitting on the doorstep with the pot and its soil and its seed, holding it, watching it, smiling.

'What are you doing?' asked her mother.

'I'm watching it', she said, 'waiting for it to grow.'

'Don't be silly', her mother laughed. 'Don't be silly.'

But the little girl sat holding the pot and the soil and its seed until bedtime.

The next day at breakfast the mother watched the little girl come down and go straight to the back door to the pot to pick it up again. She laughed again.

'You'll never have the patience to wait and watch – it'll take too long. . . .'

The little girl nodded her head vigorously. 'Yes, I will', she declared, 'I'll watch and wait for it to grow.'

After school the little girl ran home and, picking up the pot, she stared at the smooth brown soil and smiled to herself, thinking of the tiny seed tucked deep in the earth. Her mother frowned but left her alone. 'It'll soon wear off', she said.

But day after day the little girl ran home from school to hold the pot and watch, she woke from sleep each morning and went to watch the earth and wait.

'Give it a dig', said her brother, 'help it along. . . . Let me water it, get some fertiliser . . . you have to work at it, help it along. . . .'

But she shook her head – it got the rain on the door-step, it needed no digging: just the watching and the waiting.

'A watched pot never boils', laughed her father when he saw her sitting again with the earth and the seed. She laughed too but didn't let go of the pot.

Day after day she watched and waited, morning and evening and even sometimes sneaking down in the night to watch under the moon and the stars, cherishing the pot and the earth and the seed.

'You can over-protect things, you know', said her mother crossly as the little girl crouched yet again by the pot, her hands around its brim. The little girl didn't seem to hear, staring at the brown earth.

'It's probably only a grass seed or a weed', sneered her brother as she watched and waited. She shook her head but said nothing.

'This is getting ridiculous', said her father sternly. 'You waste so much time just staring and watching and waiting. I think you should be playing or helping your mother.'

Tears filled the little girl's eyes and she held the pot more tightly to her.

'Please yourself then', he grumbled, walking away, 'but nothing seems to be happening. It's just a pot of dirt.'

The months went by and the little girl guarded and cherished the pot, watching the undisturbed surface of the dark soil.

'It's all very well', said her mother, 'it may be very beautiful, whatever it is, but is it worth all this waiting and staring and watching, is anything really worth all this effort?'

And then one day she came down to breakfast and the little girl had got there first. She was standing in her nightdress by the door, holding the pot and smiling shyly into it. Her mother crossed the room and looked. She gave a little gasp, she couldn't help it.

It was exquisitely blue – tiny, fragile, barely above the surface, but exquisitely blue, a flower and a deep green leaf. The brown earth seemed to blush around the delicate gentle blossom. The earth and the circling pot seemed to be saying to the watching little girl:

'So, here you are then, what you waited for, what you were watching for. Here it is, at last, at long last.'

And all she could do was nod and smile and laugh occasionally, stare at the astonishing blue flower and laugh and smile and nod.

The Well

The little girl dipped her bucket in the water and sighed.
It was as dirty as ever, if not dirtier. The factories higher
up the river were steadily ruining the water. She looked
into the bucket as she pulled it up – grey, floating with
bits, no sparkle from the sun catching on it. She filled
her other bucket and began the slow staggering walk
back home. As always she glanced at the dense little
thicket of trees just near her home – mysterious,
intriguing, strange. She had always been warned not to
go near it – it was dangerous, frightening, impenetrable.

At home she tipped her water into the great saucepans
they used to boil the water and make it fit to use. Exhausted she went outside and sat on the step. Her eye was
drawn again to the dense thicket. Was there really anything there? Why should it be so frightening?

She stood up. As she looked she noticed that the sunlight was penetrating the thick trees in a different way
and she could see that it wasn't just trees and bushes –
there were stones there too, a structure, a space.

Without thinking about it she began to walk towards
the thicket. Reaching it it seemed quite impenetrable
again but she pushed and pulled at the branches and
soon she was clambering into the dark interior, quiet
and shadowy, dense with foliage and tangled branches.

With a little cry she stubbed her foot against a stone
and putting her hand out to stop herself falling, she
found herself leaning against a low wall. She began to

pull at the thick growth over the wall, cutting her hands as she did so, and slowly its shape emerged. It was a small round, low wall, a few feet high and only a few feet round. As she tugged at the bushes she uncovered the top too and discovered a thick stone slab.

'It's a well!' she cried to herself in astonishment. Immediately she pushed at the slab to uncover the well but it was too heavy, too long undisturbed. She stood back, gasping and exasperated. Was there water in the well? What would it be like? Would she be able to reach it?

With a yelp of exasperation she gave another push – and the great stone lid moved. . . . It moved a few inches off the top of the rim, leaving a tiny gap at the edge. Eagerly she peered in. It was pitch dark, utterly silent, but the smell was sweet. She inhaled it deeply – it seemed to come from very deep – sweet, fresh, cool.

With another wild effort she pushed again at the stone lid but there was no more movement, however hard she tried. Frustrated she peered in again, she picked up a little stick and pushed it through the crack – and listened. There was silence for a long time and then the tiniest splash, far, far away. She was convinced, when she heard it, that she also saw the sharpest, brightest, tiniest flash of water catching the stray sunlight penetrating the well.

Her mind was racing. What should she do? Who could help? Would she simply be told off for entering the thicket? She worked her way out of the bushes, thinking and wondering.

As she emerged into daylight she saw her two brothers staggering up the hill with more of the dirty water from the river. They were shocked to see her coming out of the trees and began to say so. But her excitement wouldn't be contained. She grabbed them by the arm, spilling their water as she did so, and dragged them towards the thicket. Fearfully they followed her.

'We need to get the lid off.' She declared, pushing at it already, when they had made their way through the trees. They were still staring in astonishment at the well but already they too had noticed the fresh, clean smell that had drifted up through the little crack. Together they pushed and heaved – and nothing happened. So they pushed again and now slowly, slowly the slab began to move and slide and suddenly it tipped and rolled off into the bush behind the well. Breathless, they leapt to the rim and peered in. Now, as sunlight filtered in flashes through the overshadowing trees – now they could see a distant shining glint of water. Far away, deep and remote but real and the sweet smell was stronger than ever.

A brother ran for a long rope and a clean bucket. Eagerly they tied the handle on and swung it, clanking over the side of the well. They seemed to be lowering it for ever. Then they heard the faint splash and the bucket became heavier and heavier and between them they began to haul it up. Up and up it came, soon they could see it, flashing and twinkling in the light. Six hands grabbed the handle as it reached the rim. Three mouths sipped the cold, crystal water. Their eyes shone at each other – it was the most beautiful thing they had ever tasted.

'But where did it come from?' asked their mother as she took another deep, astonished drink of the delicious water.

'We found the well in the thicket', said the little girl. 'It's very deep – but very fresh and clear.'

'And so near to us,' said their mother, 'and we never knew. No more dirty, lifeless water now,' she said, 'just this, sparkling and clear from deep, deep down.'

'I Am'

'I am alive', he said aloud. It was one of those moments
when suddenly everything was intensely real, hard, he
felt he could touch the air, the wind, the sky – feel it,
hold it – real and alive. 'I am alive', he said again. 'I am.
I am.' His voice echoed round the rocks of the mountain
gully where he'd stopped to catch his breath. It came
back to him in the breeze. 'I am. I am. I live, I breathe,
I feel, I am.' He said it aloud again to the soaring rocks. 'I
live, I breathe, I feel, I am. I am.' The affirmation circled
the rocks and rose and rose to the sky and the clouds.
He shouted it again and laughed. 'I am. I am.'

He looked up – he wanted to climb to the very top of
the mountain, far, far away in the clouds. Slowly he
turned to look back down the way he'd come: the path
wound down and down disappearing and suddenly
reappearing. Where had he come from? Still behind him
somehow he could hear the echoes – 'I am. I am alive.'
He was tingling with the power of it, he wanted to hold
on to all the effort and desire that had burst into the
energy and force of his cry to the rocks. 'I am. I live.
It's me.' All that I have been, he whispered, every bit of
me, all the life I've lived is here in this moment coming
to life, now alive, all that I remember . . . with a smile
he turned again to the rock: 'I am what I am', his voice
came back to him. He stared at the soaring stone. Where
did this surge of life come from? Where did this almost
uncontrollable, almost unbearably intense sense of

94

being lead to? This was not just himself, this little frail, fragile individual – something deeper was surging through him, something stronger and richer: was this what it means to be a human being? Was this the love of life in all its powerful urgency bursting in him? From what depths did this overwhelming desire and love of being alive come? Was this the voice of God? 'I am. I am alive. I am what I have been. I am what I am. I am.' He grinned to himself, still bubbling with this surging force, and stepped nearer to the rock craning his neck to take in all the rock face, up and up, to the blue above.

'And I will be', he shouted, slapping the rock, till it echoed.

This life was not going to end – the 'I am' was too strong in him. 'I will be', he cried again and the words spun up the rock, echoing and echoing: the sure future, a conviction of hope, life that always grows and grows. As he gazed at the sky he began to brace himself for the rest of the climb – heading for the sky, he smiled. The bursting life in him filled the way ahead with hope and longing and desire – heading for the Promised Land he thought and he knew for a moment all the intense hopes of all the living in all the ages, aching for heaven, for the kingdom of God, for a new world, for the Promised Land and Journey's End. He cried one last time to the rock – let the cry of the human spirit, the voice of God, surge through him again – 'I am. I live. I hope. There is life to hope for.' And it echoed all around him as he strode out on the upward path and with every step, his eyes on the sky above, he said 'I am. I am.'

The Void

The rock face was smooth and solid against her back as she shuffled her feet slightly to settle herself more securely on the little ledge. She breathed slowly, under control, carefully assessing. Her companion had climbed on ahead, more familiar with the rock – she was new to this, a novice. A little breeze brushed at her, warm in the sun. She looked slowly up. The rock curved round into a tight crevice, and curved away again – sheer, smooth, unapproachable. The route so far had been tiny toe-holds and tight finger grips until she reached this little ledge where she perched. The rock face fell away below her, sheer again, to boulders and rough grass and a few shrubs a long way below.

Very carefully, sure of her carefully-balanced crouching, she looked out ahead. The empty air, the space, the blue sky with its idling clouds was a dizzyness in front of her. Instinctively her palms flattened against the rock behind her till the grey stone darkened with her sweat. Now she looked up. The way ahead was into the crevice . . . her eye followed the curve of the rock upwards as it formed a chimney between the two faces and the route went up and up, straight between smooth rock until it reached a far circle of brighter sky at the top. There was no sign of her companion, of anyone, no sound at all except the ruffles of the breeze and her own steady breathing.

Carefully she slid along the ledge further into the crevice to the point where the ledge merged back into the rock. The rock encased her now. Below, the chimney dropped steadily, narrowly, until it was too dark to discern details – an abyss. And above, a few feet wide, it rose and rose smooth, straight and narrow, up to that shape of light above. Carefully she examined the curves of the rock – there were no foot or hand holds, no ledges or cracks, just the challenge, the invitation of smooth stone. The way up was to brace her back against the rock and to kick her feet against the opposite rock face and, braced between the chimney walls, to shuffle and push and work her way up and up.

She stretched out a foot from the edge of the little ledge towards the opposite face – it wouldn't reach. She looked down again into the darkness. It would take a little jump to get her feet against the rock of the opposite face – a little leap out over the emptiness below. Calmly she assessed the distance. Yes, she could reach but her breath was coming deeper now, stronger – the leap, the risk. . . . There was still no sound, no offer of help, only the silent challenge of the rock. She braced herself against the rock and looked up. She could feel the abyss within her now, a yawning space that opened below her. She concentrated on her breathing, on the rock face opposite, on her feet and legs . . . she had never done this before. She would not paralyse herself with thinking, she would acknowledge the abyss, the void, but she would look up to the light – and with another sharp breath she pushed back against the rock behind her and threw her feet towards the opposite face, out over the deep space, over nothing at all.

Even as her feet struck the rock she was asking, where does courage come from? As she felt the jolt of her legs stiffening to stabilise her she wondered where this surge within her came from, from what deep down place, past what obstacles; could she trust it? How could she know? She wondered almost aloud in the instance of the leap whether this upward surge within her could bear the risk, meet the challenge. She shuddered into a rigid body's bridge across the chasm and felt the exhilaration run through her, stretched, taut, already pushing on. She tilted her head back a little as she began to push and work and edge her way up, and out of the corner of her gleaming, triumphant eye she could keep in sight the bright and very slowly growing shape of the open sky at the very top.

The Door

She rarely went into the cellar. It was damp and dark and the steps down into it were uneven and there was nothing to hold onto. She passed the cellar door frequently, of course, in moving about her house, but mostly she hardly noticed it was there. But every so often she felt the need to open the door and go down, taking her torch, reminding herself that the cellar was part of her house too, it belonged to her and ought not to be so neglected.

Down at the bottom of the steps she looked around. It really was damp but basically tidy, some forgotten things stored away, a lot of dust and some mould. She looked around. The cellar was bigger than she remembered and stretched further back than she had ever been. Tentatively she stepped out in the direction of unknown corridors. It was very quiet except for her own deep breathing and the sound of her feet on the stone floor, the rest of the house – tidy, light and warm – seemed very far away. She carried on along the low corridor, walking more and more slowly and half deciding at every step to turn back and go no further.

Then she saw the door. It was the end of the corridor, a solid wooden door that didn't surprise her though she was sure she'd never seen it before. She sighed – she knew she had to open it, dusty and solid as it was, but she had no idea where it led.

She jerked hard at the bolts and they gave, she turned

the key and with a rusty grating it moved, she lifted the latch and heaved the door open.

She was caught with a gasp in the blast of wind as it howled suddenly round her from the open door. She couldn't move but stood gasping and staring. There was nothing there . . . below her feet, across the threshold of the door, there was nothing there, just emptiness; on either side and all above her was emptiness and nothing. It was black and endless, a void, but she stared into it, unable to move or close the door. The wind continued to blast its way around her – the only sound was the howling in her ears of this cold draught from nowhere and from nothing. Yet it was not frightening or horrible so much as absolutely nothing at all. Her home above seemed so very far away, so unreal, so artificial in the face of this blank, this emptiness – and yet that same home opened into this. She stared and stared, dismayed, shocked, paralysed. She knew she had to do something – she knew she could step through the door into the void, she knew it would take her, and she knew she could close the door and shut out the wind again, return to her cellar, up the stairs to her home – warmth and light and safety. What should it be?

She took a deep breath, inhaling the wind from the emptiness, and closed the door.

'Yes'

'Yes', he said, 'yes, I will, yes.'

Nothing had changed in front of him – the waterfall still tumbled into the pool between the steep rocks on either side, the rowan tree still leaned, green and waving lightly, over the other side of the pool, the pool still settled quickly – away from the waterfall – into deep and dark, tranquil water. He gazed around from his seat on the rock and traced the little path that wound its steep way up the side of the tumbling water, disappearing over the top edge, he didn't know where. No, nothing had changed and yet he had said 'yes'. Something had asked a question of him and there had been a surging up inside of him, an opening, a release – he had said 'yes' to something.

But what? There had been no Voice, no booming thunder, not even a whisper, but he had been asked a question – a question that must be answered and he had said 'yes'. He knew that, as he sat there, he could have said 'no', could have turned away, could have refused. And nothing would have changed – the waterfall, the tree, the path, the pool would still have been there – and yet it would all have been duller, dimmer, sadder. . . . But he had said 'yes'. What did it mean? What would he have to do? He didn't know that either but knew that the world was alive now for him, that life was a gift he had taken with both hands, that he had said 'yes' to a destiny, a way ahead, a path over the edge.

'Yes', he said again, this time aloud, 'yes, I will. Yes.'

Contemplating

He pulled his hood more firmly round his ears as the wind scooped the rain into his face. He pressed forward, his head down, and then paused, breathing hard, by a low wall. He stooped down for some shelter and tried to look around. There was no path as such, just the tight cropped grass with its tiny flowers fading out into the rocks and then the rocks jutting out and down towards the sea. He wondered if there was a storm building up. It hadn't even been raining when he left the cottage. Now the wind was blowing hard, the rain was beginning to slant into him and he wondered if he should simply stagger back. He patted his binoculars under his coat; he wasn't going to see many birds in this anyway. . . .

He stood up again, feeling the strength of the wind but he saw also the stirring of the waves and the deep blue swell of ocean stretching out ahead of him from the island and with a smile at his own folly, he pushed against the wind and onto the rocks for a last look at the mesmerising sea. He stretched and let the rain hit him as he gazed over the whipped up water. And then he noticed a step in the rocks and, just below him, the door to a long low shelter of rough stone. A hide.

He scrambled down towards it and slid open the little door. The narrow interior simply had a bench and, opposite it, an opening in the crude stonework that ran the length of the hide, sheltered slightly by the overhang of the roof. He was alone, it smelled of earth and sea, it cut out little of the weather's noise but changed it, framing it in the empty window. He sat on the bench and pushed his hood back. The hide looked out across the promontory of rock towards the open sea, towards rocks out to sea where seals might bask in different weather. Perfectly sighted for watching birds as they flew in from the sea, as they searched for food in the rocks, even – higher up – where they might nest. He could wait and watch, he thought, quite unnoticed – waiting and watching. A place of observation, he thought, and leaned on the low parapet watching the rain, the rocks, the waves, the sky.

Slowly his breath settled into a slower rhythm. The wind and rain seemed to settle too and he stared at the sea, the heaving of the ocean, the regular crashing of the waves, its surges against the rocks. He did see an occasional, rare bird flutter desperately against the wind but mostly it was the water and the rock and the sky he watched, feeling their rhythm like his own breathing. He smiled as if he were becoming part of it, joining its movement, its flow – making a single nature.

'I shall have to come here again', he thought, 'a hiding place – a place for observation, for contemplating.'

NOTE: The Latin word 'temple' comes from the word for an 'observatory', a 'place for observations' – it's at the heart of our word 'contemplation'.

Yellow

He had dreamed yellow.

He woke, immediately wide awake, his mind full of the colour. Great bands of fierce, bright yellow had spun slowly in his head. They hung above him and around him, moving, vast, flat shining rectangles of yellow.

He lay in bed eagerly gathering the memories of his dream.

What sort of yellow was it? It was yellow like the sun, saffron, like sunflowers, like buttercup, like the tip of a flame. It was not pale or pastel, not pretty or subdued but fierce, strong, full of the light, as bright as life. His mind ran on with more comparisons as he rose and dressed – every shade of yellow he saw required a comparison: 'No, not as pale as that. . . . Yes, something like that. . . .'

He was in the studio at the bottom of his garden for days after that. His friends called and he smiled and told them he was painting again. 'Can we see?' they asked him, but he shook his head. 'Not yet', he said, 'but soon. . . .'

'But what are you painting?' they asked.

'A colour', he said.

'Just a colour?' they said.

'The beauty is all that matters', he said, 'that's all.'

He was shut up a few more days and then he invited his friends round to see. They came into the little studio and gazed. The walls were hung with square and rec-

tangular boards and canvasses of every shape and size –
from floor to ceiling, small ones, horizontal and vertical,
narrow and broad, thick wooden planks and fluttering
pieces of cloth. And they were all yellow. There were
variations of shade but not a wide range. It was as if
the painter had been on a search for a very particular
yellow and here were the last stages of the quest. There
was nothing on the paintings but sheer yellow, yellow
everywhere, band after band, painting after painting.
The effect was dazzling, breathtaking – yellow after
yellow after yellow.

'It's like walking into the sun', said one.

'So warm, such energy . . .' said another.

'Like dreaming', murmured a third.

'Beauty is all that matters', said the painter, unable
to take his eyes off the yellow. 'Beauty.'

Into the Sea

'You can't do that.' They said.

'But it's so negative.' They said.

'You wouldn't have the courage, in any case.' They scoffed.

'It would be such a waste.'

'You have no right', they said, 'you're not in control.'

The smile had not gone from his face all the time he had talked to them and still now, as he sat in the wispy grass of the dunes watching the sea, he was smiling.

It was a beautiful day. The very lightest breeze was drifting through the sand and grass and flicking over the sea. The waves were rolling gently in, the sound rhythmic, the spray sun-lit. In the sky the few clouds framed the warm, welcoming sun. The sky shone blue.

He got up and went to stand at the water's edge. There was no one else about. He felt content, his mind clear, his eyes sharp. As he stared at the sea and the sky he felt part of it, a continuity, in his place. His smile broadened.

'Well,' he said to himself, taking a long, deep breath, 'here goes. . . .'

He bent to take off his shoes and socks and placed them neatly on a rock. Then he turned and walked slowly into the sea, towards the sun. The water was colder than he expected and he laughed at himself but waded on, the waves curling up and taking his breath away as he went deeper and deeper.

A last wave broke over his head and then there was only the sea with the sun on it, the sky with its clouds and the little breeze.

The sea said:

A life is part of the universe. And so is a death.
Everything returns to the flow.
Sometimes you must rage against the waves,
sometimes you can move with their rhythm.
Sometimes the moment comes, you have a choice,
you rise up into the movement of it all.
You do have a place but you are only part of life,
  you are unique but you are invited to be part of
  the flow.
  The sea accepts you – the sun and sky welcome
  you – and the waves flow on undisturbed.

The Gardener

The sun rose. It was a beautiful day. The gardener awoke
and she smiled. It was a beautiful day – a perfect day
for gardening.

She washed and dressed and went through the door
into the garden. She stood still. It was very still. The
sun caught the dew that shone on the grass, the air
caught the wakening birds, the breeze caught the smell
of lilac. She breathed in deeply and stepped onto the
grass. Stooping she put her hand in the wetness of
the dew –

'Good morning', she greeted the grass and with a
ripple the grass returned her greeting. As she stood up
she took in all the green grass of the garden – a stroke
of genius to cover the earth with such a lovely colour.

Well, today, she decided, she wouldn't cut the grass.
She took off her shoes and walked through the dew.
There were colours everywhere – the garden blossomed
all around her. She came to the row of rose-bushes –
neat, elegant and beautiful. She bent her head to smell
the yellow flowers. She bowed to their charm and beauty
– not too many of them, not overgrown. She would not
prune the roses today. With a rustle of the breeze the
row of rose-bushes returned a bow to her.

The sun, a little higher, caught the fine outline of a
spider's web stretched across the privet hedge – she
lifted her hand to brush it away but stopped and, smiling, turned it into a salute instead. She wouldn't destroy

the spider's web today, and nodding to the spider, she crossed the lawn. The privet hedge ran along the whole garden and, if she had noticed, the gardener would have seen that it held and supported – leaf to leaf – a thousand shining webs.

She sat down on the bench beneath the oak tree. Looking up the sun greeted her through its waving branches and leaves. The birds nestled in its branches. She could feel the solid trunk behind her and reaching back she embraced it – for a moment she could feel all its life reaching up from the earth, up, up into branches and leaves, all the life flowing back from sun and rain and air down through the tree to her. The tree's branches arched right over her and touched the house. But today she would not be cutting branches from the tree – let it grow. Today it could go on growing.

In the corner of the lawn clustered a host of daisies – little, ordinary flowers opening to greet the day, bunched together, making the ground white. She smiled, the mower would cut them away – but not today. Today they would stay together, open to the sun. They brushed her feet as she walked through them, treading as lightly as she could.

'Aha', she said to herself as she knelt down by the border, 'a weed.' Today she would do the weeding. But as she touched the lush green growth she felt a strange sense of pity – even this was alive, a growing, living thing. 'Like me', she said and smiled. She let the weeds go – not today. Today she would let it all grow, today she would simply enjoy the life in it all.

She sat back in the grass that was still damp. Her hands filled with the warm brown earth and she looked around – she could feel all the life flowing. She patted the earth. 'Good morning', she said to the earth, 'not even digging today. Today the gardener is just going to be part of the garden, growing and alive. A perfect day for gardening,' she smiled and drew in a deep breath, 'a perfect day for this sort of gardening.'

The sun rose a little higher and all the garden seemed to nod and wave and bow and rustle in greeting to her.

The Island

The boat lurched as the currents changed and the swell suddenly deepened. They had rounded the headland and were heading out across the straits. The water raced and roared in great green mountains that sparkled in the sunlight before they rippled massively on under the stern of the plunging boat. They seemed for whole moments at a time to be flung completely clear of the water as it formed a trough beneath them, before they hit again the next crest and surged through it.

She clung on in astonished fascination, entranced by the heaving sea, reassured by the nonchalant skipper, equally terrified and powerfully drawn by the sense of such fathoms below, the encircling acres of water, the roaring ocean, the tiny boat, the blue sky and the sun.

The green water heaved in its ragged huge rhythm ahead but in its trough she glimpsed another green mountain – still, fixed and slowly growing. The island. She glanced at the others for confirmation and they nodded. It was where they were going. It was swallowed again in the massive swell but the boat plunged on and in each cresting the great curve of the green slopes loomed steadily closer, caught in the uninterrupted sun, crisp shadows of the rocks and caves, tiny, distant scrambling sheep, swooping, calling gulls.

The single slope of the whole mountain-island seemed to fall sheer into the sea. The narrowest tracks trailed back and forth on the precipitous face. Only the very top seemed to curve more gently, an even richer green, the rocks turned fully upwards into the sun. Through the still heaving sea, from the swooping boat, she gazed, awed and entranced.

Now they rounded the headland of the island and slowly the water quietened a little, out of the great swell. Now she could see the island's gentler face, the grass swept more smoothly down to level fields and softer slopes, to small bays and wave-trapping inlets, coves, beaches. But all alight still in the full warm sun.

The boat turned sharply into a smooth-surfaced harbour inlet and suddenly the land leapt towards her. They had reached the island.

The Fair Child

'Don't go', I said as I watched him stand up. He always crouched there, on the very edge, in the corner of my eye.

'I don't want you to go.' I said again looking at him directly. He stood still, a small, fair-haired boy, his hands in his pockets, looking at me.

'I have to go', he said nodding quietly.

'Please don't leave me', I said. He looked at me again. Everybody else seemed to have disappeared already.

He turned a little, looking towards the darkness beyond the edge, though some light seemed to catch still in his fair hair. He glanced back again over his shoulder.

'I have to go when the dream is ended,' he said. 'It'll be all right.'

'No', I said, more emphatically than I meant to, 'I want you to stay.'

He turned fully until I was facing only his back though he didn't walk any further off.

'I have to go', he said again. 'You'll be all right.'

'This time', I said, stepping towards him, 'stay this time, for the first time, stay with me. . . .'

He wasn't always there. Sometimes I barely glimpsed him before he was gone. Sometimes he spoke, joined in, laughed and played: more often he sat, crouched, at the very edge, watching – without a name I could remember, but familiar.

He didn't turn round.

'But where will I go when you wake?' he asked and his question echoed out of the darkness he was facing.

'Just don't leave me anymore', I urged, reaching out to take hold of his little arm. He let me turn him round but, small as he was, I knew it was his will not my strength that let him face me again. He could have flicked me away like dust from his sleeves, he could have disappeared over the edge into the darkness.

There was something surging in my ears, an upward rushing. I tried to hold him more tightly, staring into his solemn, small face. 'Oh no', I murmured, 'don't let me leave you. I don't want to go . . . keep hold of me.'

My feet were leaving the ground, there was a warm, clear push upwards all around me like rising through green depths towards the light. I could not hold onto him anymore as I was lifted upwards. He was looking upwards now and smiling, watching me. He took his hand out of his pocket and waved once. He grew smaller, fainter, as the light increased. Then, a last time, there was just a voice. 'I have to go. Everything will be all right.'

Forest

It seemed endless from where he stood, green, deep, endless. Thin shafts of light slid among the trees nearest to him but soon the dense rows cut out the light and it seemed to stretch into an ever-darker remoteness. He stood still. He leaned against the nearest pine and put his head back to look up its straightness into the greenness above. He could see no sky, it felt like being under water, but not refreshing, not moving. He peered up into the twining branches, locked with those of surrounding trees. Nothing moved. He could touch the trunks of the surrounding trees, they were so close, the bark brittle and rough. Pieces flaked off and dropped into the crisp, dry bed of needles and cones and faded vegetation at his feet, around the roots of all these trees. All those roots, he thought. He stared at the brown litter of the ground, he felt alone, lonely. Everything was brittle, dry, nothing was moving. The light was weak, the distance so dark, he could so easily be lost. He looked up from the ground and an empty space seemed to rise too and spread inside him, fragile, lifeless, drained, so that even his mouth suddenly seemed dry and empty. He stared into the distant darknesses, weary as the forest, dry and lifeless as the trees. His chin sank back on his chest and he stared again, unseeing, at the ground.

Then the forest stirred. A rustle, a flicker, a gesture. He didn't notice it the first time but it stirred again. He realised he could smell the rich, dark edges of the pine.

115

A breeze had drifted through the trees. It had stirred
the branches so that they waved a moment's fragrance
through the airless spaces – and he caught it. He looked
up. As he did the forest stirred again in the breeze. The
shafts of light shifted and grew and changed, green
and shades of brown, sliding over trunks and leaves and
cones – the distant darkness remained but seemed to
shimmer a little, to surge and stir. It was still again but
only for a moment and the breeze returned. This time
he felt it on his face. It was gentle and warm. It was like
someone's sweet breath, not urgent or demanding or
even powerful, simply alive and warm. It picked up a
little so that the forest was gently responding to its light
breathing. Leaves turned faces up into waving light,
branches swayed slightly against other swaying
branches, a cone fell in a smooth curve to the rustling
earth. And now the forest could be heard – the soft
swishing of leaves, the creak of a branch, a light whistling, a gentle rushing, a rhythm of breathing. He was
mesmerised, entranced, he felt drawn into this living –
reaching and stretching with the trees of the forest for
all that the breeze was bringing, for what was being
breathed through the woods. He took a deep breath himself, savouring the scents of the forest, filling the empty
spaces. This was not the breath of loneliness or of something lost, it was not an empty breeze. It was laden
with other scents and hopes and possibilities, spirit from
somewhere else but making the forest now alive, making
him now alive. So he stood up straight, so he gazed into
the gently shifting distance of the forest, so he opened
his mouth and breathed, breathing longer and deeper
than ever he had breathed before.

The Waterfall

She had slept but now she lay awake in her sleeping bag, listening. The tent was still, without a breeze to ripple the canvas, the only sound was the waterfall. Its thunder rolled on as it had rolled all night while she slept – as it had always thundered, a roar, an unmodulated sound of falling. She stared at the tent roof but the sight didn't register – all that registered was the descending cascade of water, drumming in her ears. She had pitched the tent on the little grassy outcrop part way up the side of the fall. Looking up she could see the sudden curve of water as it hit empty space and dropped down the sheer rock face. Below the outcrop it fell further still to the dark pool far below, the deep rock echoing the end of the waters' vast descent. The river below – for all its depth and force – was too far away to be heard in the tent. The river above, broad and rushing over rocks and boulders, was also too far away to be heard as it gathered for its unexpected falling. In the tent the only sound was the unending cascade, the all-obliterating, all-embracing roar of falling water. She listened for the variations in the sound, the catching of a rock, the tumbling of a broken branch, but her ears drew her deeper into the continuous thunder, the sound that would never end. She closed her eyes so that the waterfall took over her senses, it was falling in her mind. It thundered on. From its high ridge of rock it fell through her without violence but immersing her, saturating her. It drummed and echoed in every corner of her, a vibration, a solemn and deep humming, its register low and continuous so that she felt it through every cell — echoing from before its first flooding, reverberating through every pool and meander, every widening of the river, every reaching for the ocean. The echoing water fell and fell. It was the sound of the universe.

The Tree

It was absolutely and perfectly still and yet to him the tree seemed almost to vibrate with life. From the chair in his room – or from the bed – it filled the window, a dense, rich green, its branches fanning out to hold on to the sun. Pine cones stood upright on its bending arms, proud, heavy with seeds. Way below the dark trunk spread into the ground and he thought of the roots reaching down through the earth – dark, silent, gathering life.

The tree reached out over the red-tiled roof of the old chapel just below his window, the gutters filled with the tree's needles. Between the reaching branches – like a frame – he could see across the wide valley to a misty view of distant mountains and all below in the haze the villas and villages of Tuscany. The tree seemed to hold them too – and all the colours and shades of the sky and all the heat and dust of the ground.

It began to rain. The tree stirred and while the running water bowed its branches it seemed to reach still for the life in the rain, for the coolness, for the refreshment. The rain deepened the colours of the tree as it dripped and soaked along its branches. The green shadows in amongst the needles and branches were stirring dark and somehow deeper in the tree. The water soaked down onto the trunk making it black and streaked, rain dripped from the branch ends on to the chapel roof making the tiles shine and the gutters flow.

He watched the rain weigh steadily on the branches so that they shone too and slowly hung down more and more, moving lightly with the weight of the dripping rain. But the tree was not hanging down, it was up, reaching, stretching out, alive, gathering the rain, remembering the sun, preparing the seeds.

Other Horizons

He stood at the bottom of the mountain and looked up, there was a track snaking upwards from just above him but he contemplated the heather and the gorse and the bracken that covered the slopes and thought he could go straight up. Further up, right up at the top, the sky was stark blue, outlining the smooth curve of the mountain's peak. Clouds sped by in the breeze and disappeared beyond his horizon. He began to climb.

It wasn't a great mountain, it was an island rising from the spreading ocean, but it was a real mountain, rock and heather and scree and he wanted to stand on its peak. He climbed, leaning towards the grass and bracken and the thick heather – he loved the feel of it brushing his legs, filling his hands when it was steep enough to scramble. He paused, already breathing hard and looked up, the horizon had changed little, the clouds still speeding by, the blue fierce and stark. But he looked behind him and there everything was changed. The little island sloped gently into the sea and now he was high enough to see it all, the rock edges meeting the breaking waves, the wide, wide circle of the sea in every direction, the flecks of white in the breeze and even what must be the occasional seal. He sighed with pleasure and went on climbing, stooped into the mountain-side, sensing the vast solidity of the rock beneath him. Towards the top he stopped again, breathing harder now. He looked up – it seemed the same, that curve of rock against the blue.

He was suddenly frustrated, even angry and kicked against a boulder which wobbled and rocked and then rolled gently a few feet down the mountain-side. He was looking back again and once again the horizon had changed – now he could see what seemed like the far edges of the ocean as they met the blue of the sky. Away to one side he could see the headland of the mainland but in the other direction it was all lightly heaving ocean and waves. He rested a while and noticed the circling birds and the small flowers clinging to the mountain-side, he felt for a moment like them, glad of the solid earth, reaching up, alive.

He went on up and the ground levelled a little and suddenly he was on top. On top of the world it seemed, full of far horizons in the fading sun, breathtaking in the breeze. He turned slowly to take it all in – receding mountains on the mainland ahead, the circle of the sea in every other direction, a boat – tiny, far below – birds and the still-speeding clouds. He looked towards the west where the low sun silhouetted the far-away ridges of distant mountains on the horizon of the sea. The low sun was casting long shadows and over his shoulder he saw his own elongated shadow disappearing over the edge of the mountain: he wondered where it ended but didn't look for the steepness of the place.

He breathed deeply. He was on top of the mountain. Already night was creeping in from the east but he sat to watch rather than retreating and soon there were stars scattering across the ever-darkening blue. He placed his hands flat on the rock below him and seemed to feel the mountain preparing for the night. He leaned his head in his hands. He was on top of the mountain.

Stone

The small boy drew back his arm and with a gasp of effort he flicked the flat smooth stone out in a low curving arc across the water until it lightly touched the surface of the pool and skimmed once, twice, three, four times, before vanishing with a 'ploop' below the surface. The boy grinned with delight and turned through the trees to run, rustling through the bracken and the undergrowth to find the path again and disappear into the trees. The ducks that had squawked into flight at the skimming of the stone, dropped with a splash onto the water again, rippling the pool into wavelets. The trees and the rushes round the edge of the secluded pool waved and bowed a little in a gentle intermittent breeze and then rustled into stillness again. Another bird called loudly and dipped and disappeared into the lush trees at the far edge of the pool.

The stone slid gently through the water, down, deep through the lightly wafting weeds, out of the filtering sun and into the silent watery shade, and came softly to rest on the bottom. A frond of weed waved and was still again. The tiny fish that had sped in every direction as the stone broke the surface, slowly returned, circling, drifting, darting with little flashes of sunlight on the shining scales. A little shimmer of sand from the bed below the stone drifted in the clear water and gently settled.

Up above, the broken surface slowly settled until the

trees and rushes were mirrored green again with the blue sky in the bright sun. The breeze seemed to hold its breath as everything gently settled and for a moment – just a long moment – everything was absolutely still.

Voice

'Not yet, not yet', said the Voice inside of her as she looked up the road ahead. It rose through the trees until it was out of sight so that she wondered if this was the last hill. She strode on.

'Is this the last hill?' asked the old man who leaned on her arm, 'are we nearly there?'

She didn't answer but put her hand over his on her arm to help him up the sloping road.

'Oh, my feet ache', he said, 'I'm not as agile as I used to be. . . .' She wanted to say that her feet ached as well but she simply smiled at him and patted his hand and helped him on.

'Will we see it from the top of this hill?' he asked, breathing heavily and looking up long enough to take in the brow of the road.

'Maybe', she said, 'keep hoping. . . .'

Slowly they climbed the last yards to the top and stopped, catching their breath. In front of them the road wound on and down, rising again in the far distance – on and on, through woods and fields, disappearing from sight every so often, reappearing further on, deeper in to the country, narrower and narrower until it reached the horizon.

'Oh', said the old man as they stood and gazed at the road, 'it must be over those next hills then . . .' and he began to walk slowly on again. She let him go and gazed down the winding road.

'This is the road to all you desire', said the Voice inside of her as she watched the old man struggling on, 'this is the road of longing and hope.'

She set off, walking a little faster to catch up with the old man, and reaching him she took his arm and helped him on.

'It's a long road', he said, his eyes staring ahead at the far horizon, 'but we'll get there soon. . . .'

They walked on in silence for some time.

'I dream of the City', the old man said, 'it's going to be so beautiful, so full of lovely people, so happy, so peaceful, so perfect. . . .'

'The road is beautiful too', she said.

'Oh yes', he agreed looking round and noticing the trees and the fields and the following sky, as if for the first time.

'The road is beautiful too', echoed the Voice inside of her and for a while she was content with the steady walk and the winding track and the changing horizon.

The road wound on and the day went by and the sky began to change as dusk began to fall. The old man began to stumble and walk more and more slowly, his feet dragging, his pain growing.

'I ache so much', he said. Her own feet were aching too but she tried to comfort him and to keep going.

'We'll get there soon', she said, 'every road comes to an end – and then we shall be there. . . .'

'Yes', he said, 'in the City, we shall have arrived . . . oh, but I ache so much.'

She looked at his fragile, struggling body and felt her own aching and pain and was filled with a deep longing. 'You must bring your fragility with you', said the Voice inside of her and she gripped his arm the more tightly and smiled at him in encouragement in the growing dark and began to tell him stories and jokes as they slowly walked on under the moon, through the deepening night.

When the night was at its darkest and most silent, and they seemed to have been walking for ever and could see nothing ahead, when they ached and their feet dragged and nothing kept them going but each other, the old man said, 'I don't think I can go on. . . .'

'Think of the City', said the Voice inside of her.

'Think of the City', she repeated and began to try to describe to him its beauty and its wonders and its peace.

He nodded, struggling along beside her, 'All I ever wanted', he sighed, 'what I dreamed about, my heart's desire. . . .'

For a long while then they were silent, walking on, following the dark windings of the road, on and on, the pain was a little numbed, the road a little less unending, the hope a little brighter. And as they walked the sky began to brighten and slowly, oh so slowly, the day began to dawn.

'Not yet', said the Voice inside of her again, 'not yet – but soon.'

As the daylight grew and the sun began to rise, as they felt their aching a little relieved by the warming of the sun, the road began to climb again, up and up to a curving brow. Breathing hard, the old man looked and his pace quickened, dragging his aching feet. 'It must be now', he said, 'we must be there . . . the end of the road.' He broke free from her arm and she watched him struggle ahead of her up the hill, driven by hope and desire. . . . She watched him as the road got steeper as he battled on, staying ahead, breathing hard, on and up. Then she stopped because she saw him stop as he reached the brow of the hill and she heard his long low sigh and she saw him slowly raise and stretch his arms as if for an embrace and she heard him say:

'There it is; at last, at last. . . .' With a gasp she ran to catch him up – and there it was.

Spread out on the plain before them, stretching for miles within its circling walls, the glowing City, the most beautiful sight she had ever seen. It shone with colour and light, its buildings and towers, old and new, caught the morning sun, its streets were full of people, some of them were even emerging already to greet the new arrivals, there were trees and streams everywhere and a great slow river through the middle.

'It's perfect', said the old man, his eyes shining, 'it really is perfect . . . all that I ever desired, all that I ever hoped for.'

She smiled and gazed and gazed at the beautiful sight, more than she could desire, greater than all her longing.

'You have arrived', said the Voice inside of her, 'but don't forget the Road you came on.'

She turned to tell the old man, her companion, but he was gone, he was running, his aching transformed, his weakness changed by the sight of the city, he was running down the little hill, eager to greet the citizens who came to meet him. With a skip in her step and a smile she began to run as well.

The Maze

He paused a moment in front of the high hedge. It was neat and carefully cut, it stretched just above his head, and it reached out on either side in a long straight green line. He had never been in a maze before but now he headed purposefully towards the only opening in the wall of green and passed between the tall, leafy ends of the hedge. He paused, finding himself standing in a small, colourful garden of flowers and shrubs with little paths that led into the hedges beyond. It was deliciously quiet and each path was inviting and enticing. The hedge opposite was lower than the outer wall and arches and trellises opened to let the paths deeper into the maze. He smiled, acknowledging that his choice of path was a matter of luck and he set out along the middle one and the arch into the maze. But immediately he was surrounded by green privet walls around a square of grass: there was no exit here. He checked the hedges carefully but there was no way out except the way he had come in. So he retraced his steps into the first garden to start again. This time the path he chose led into a long straight passage between low hedges, in the distance it turned a corner and he set off towards it. As he walked he looked over the hedges on either side. All that seemed to be in sight were more hedges of different heights, stretching endlessly, until on his left a gleam caught his eye. He stopped to look. It seemed to be a pole, white and shining, standing up, bright in the afternoon sun against a deep blue sky. He watched it for a moment and began slowly walking on, keeping the white point in his eye. It must mark the way through the maze, he decided and he thought he would not let it out of his sight. On he strolled as the path curved to the left and the white point stayed with him. The bend in the path brought him to a choice of ways through the hedge and he debated which would take him nearer to the white pole. He tried the first but instantly the hedges were too high to see over and he wanted to see the white marker. He stepped back through the opening and tried instead the third opening. The path ran at right angles to the gateway and the hedge opposite was cut in a wave of high and low curves. He saw immediately that this meant the pole was regularly in sight as the hedges dipped. Should he go left or right? The gleam of white was to the left so he began to follow as the path curved, turned sharply and twisted. At first the pole was hardly out of sight as the hedge rose and fell, then gradually the high curves became longer and higher and the white point was out of sight for longer and longer periods. He found himself hurrying slightly and looking anxiously in the narrow dips for the reassuring point – but it was still there.

The path swung on and began to give him more cho-ices, more doorways and openings, but he kept his eye on the shining point. Occasionally he made a mistake and it was lost to sight beyond walls of green. Once or twice a touch of panic reached him as he gazed around and every direction seemed the same and sometimes he felt he had been in some of the clearings many times already. A wave of lostness surged in him for a moment as turning and turning he searched for the white and shining point. Then he found it and with a sigh made off

– almost running now – along the path where he could
see it most clearly.

On he trod, selecting carefully openings and paths and
hoping now, at any moment, to be through and free from
these green walls and neat grass paths, these curving
hedges and enigmatic openings.

The path began to widen and he came to the highest
hedge of all with three openings. Tentatively he tried
them all. Only in the third could he glimpse the white
point still standing sharp against the sky. He followed
it. And now there was fragrance too, the smell of roses
– and as he made his way along the green, curving path
there was a sound too, the sound of falling water, regular
and measured like a fountain might sound. He walked a
little more quickly anticipating the end – the fragrances
grew stronger and the sound of water louder and the
white pole brighter and clearer. The path curved suddenly to the left and he stopped, his breath taken away.
Through an arch in the hedge was a sunlit garden full
of roses and flowers of every colour, neat and carefully
tended, they surrounded a large white fountain that was
gently spraying jets of water into the air so that they
tumbled and cascaded down over large, brimming dishes
of stone. All this caught his eye and made him sigh but
most astonishing of all was the creature sitting perfectly
still in front of the fountain.

It was a unicorn – greater than a horse but graceful,
elegant, it was shining white, its flanks were powerful
but still as it sat unmoving, its great horn rising into
the fountain-shining air. With a laugh of surprise it
dawned on him that that was the shining point that he
had made his guide. Still the great creature sat perfectly
quiet and unmoving so that he wondered if it were a
statue. He stepped into the garden, admiring the beauty

of the animal, refreshed by the fragrances, enjoying the
moist air from the fountain. Very slowly and gracefully
the unicorn rose to its feet and lifted its head solemnly
to shake its thick white mane. The horn glinted and
shone and gleamed, catching the fountain's water in
the sunlight. Slowly the creature turned and walked –
soundless on the grass – around the fountain, its horn
still bright and shining as it moved away. Slowly it
passed through a large opening in the hedge beyond the
roses and slowly, as it went, it lowered its head as if to
point still. The hedge opened onto a flight of steps and
there at the top was the house from which he had set
off. With a smile he followed the unicorn.

Darkness

The little boy did not know how long he had been there. The darkness had taken away even his sense of time. It was just so dark. He was sitting on the ground, though he couldn't see it, and staring at the dark. He turned his head slowly round but there was absolutely nothing to see but black space – deep, thick, black space. He remembered his terror earlier on, his panic and confusion, the deep sense of being on his own . . . but now that all seemed a long way off, it was so long ago. Now he simply saw the darkness and he sat and he waited. He lifted his hand again to his face – as he had done a thousand times now – and he looked and he waved his fingers and saw nothing, nothing whatsoever, however near he brought his fingers to his eyes. He blinked again, very deliberately, but there was nothing there, nothing blocking his eyes, his eyes were not accidently closed – there was simply no light whatsoever and nothing therefore but this inky, velvet-like depth of darkness. He stared. It was not a wall but a presence, everywhere. It was so terrifying and yet he sighed – it was empty too, nothing came to him from it so what should he fear? He just waited, alone, invisible to himself, everything invisible to him. He waited.

After a long time – another long time, he seemed to have been there so long – he put his hands on the ground, the only solid thing he knew, and pushed himself to his feet. It was a long time since he had cried, sobbing and screaming in panic against the deep dark, but now tears

133

were gathering in his eyes again. Not tears of anguish this time but the quiet tears of loneliness and longing. As the tears slid down his face he stretched out his hands as far as they would go, out into the darkness, reaching – longing – every nerve and bone in his stretching arms alive with desire against the dark. With a little sigh he realised that his hand had slipped into another hand.

He was not frightened or even somehow surprised, he didn't attempt to pull away. He let his reaching hand stay there. It was a larger hand than his own, warm but rough. It held him lightly but firmly, cupped in the palm. He held on and waited. He didn't think to speak but strained instead, against all expectation, to see through the blanket of night the hand, the arm, the person. He stared and felt the hand – and went on staring against the dark. The hand was rough with scars he realised after holding it a long time, its lightness was because of its own pain as well as the boy's. The boy drew in a deep breath and clutched the hand more tightly – he was suddenly filled with pity for this person with the gentle, holding hands. He relaxed his clutch but held it still. Slowly it dawned on him that they were moving now – steadily, slowly pressing forward together, walking through the pitch thickness of the dark. The density of the blackness never changed which made it impossible to sense the movement in any normal way – where were they going? What were they walking on? Who was leading who? He didn't know, he felt the hand in his – not pulling him, or pushing, but with him, in his.

Still no one spoke, still there was nothing but the dark to see, still they were moving together forward, on and on. The hand in his was warm and comforting but it didn't seem strong or in control. As they walked on –

134

slowly, carefully – it began to occur to him that, maybe, he was the one doing the leading and guiding, that the hand in his wanted him as much as he needed it. He stared again through the dark to see the person he was with, but there was nothing.

On they went – nothing changed, there was no sound, there was only the feeling of moving together alongside in the empty presence of the dark, the feeling of hands touching, the scars and the little fingers – and nothing else but the dark.

And then he realised they were going up. The ground below them was climbing and together the effort was greater to move forward – the hands helping each other. Now he was even less sure if he was pulling or being pulled, guiding or being guided, helping or being helped. But it was up now – still dark beyond any seeing – but up and up.

And now at last the going up was aimed at a speck of fierce light ahead. He stared unbelieving and clasped the hand tightly as it squeezed him. He realised he was staring through tears again as the speck expanded to a ring, a circle, a hole filled with light, growing bigger as they pressed towards it. He was panting and crying and staring with all the determination he could find. And the light grew brighter and bigger and nearer.

He was running, gasping, laughing and crying, running for the light. The hand in his held him more loosely, with him at first and then suddenly slipping away but with a final push to the little boy towards the brightening light. The boy half turned as he ran to see if the light would show his companion but the dazzle was as blinding as the dark and he saw nothing. But on he ran, on towards the light, his hands stretched out now to grasp the brightness that was coming.

Acknowledgements

'All Shall Be Well' was first published as 'There is nothing to be afraid of' in the *Church Times*, 13 January 1995; 'What is Spirituality?' was first published in *Movement: The Magazine of the Student Christian Movement*, Issue No. 84, Summer 1993; 'The Body of Christ' was first published in *Cutting Edge: The Theological Journal of Sheffield Chaplaincy for Higher Education*, Issue No. 12, July 1995.

Thanks are due to the following publishers for permission to quote copyright material: Bloodaxe Books for the extract by R S Thomas taken from *Counterpoint*; Faber & Faber Ltd for extracts from 'The Dry Salvages' taken from *Four Quartets* by T S Eliot, 'The Arrival of the Bee Box' by Sylvia Plath and extracts from 'Lullaby' taken from *Collected Poems* by W H Auden.